Astrology

FOR BEGINNERS

Geoffrey Cornelius, Maggie Hyde and Chris Webster

Edited by Richard Appignanesi

ICON BOOKS

Published in 1995 by Icon Books Ltd.,
52 High Street, Trumpington, Cambridge CB2 2LS

Distributed in the UK, Europe and Asia by the Penguin Group:
Penguin Books Ltd, 27 Wrights Lane, London W8 5TZ

Published in Australia in 1996 by Allen & Unwin Pty. Ltd.,
PO Box 8500, 9 Atchison Street, St. Leonards, NSW 2065

Originating editor: Richard Appignanesi

ISBN 1 874166 26 9

Printed and bound in Great Britain by
The Bath Press, Avon

ASTROLOGY

the experience and interpretation of correspondence between the natural and human worlds below and the heavens above

In some shape or form astrology appears in virtually every culture of the world. It connects mythology, astronomy, mathematics, numerology, philosophy, prophecy and religion. It has been part of the intellectual vocabulary of the learned élite in many ages other than our own. It is older than science and shows no signs of going away. In its appearance as star-signs in newspapers and magazines, it is just as widespread and popular as ever.

But we cannot ignore the hostility that astrology attracts.

Guide to this Book

So what's it all about and why the controversy? We're going to look at the subject mainly as it developed in Europe and the West to find out where it's at and where it's going.

PART I: The Big Idea

Sky Consciousness at the Dawn of History

It's an illusion to judge the knowledge of ancient civilizations from **our** separation of astronomy, astrology and astro-mythology.

Take Stonehenge, which is amongst the most impressive of the stone-age observatories. On midsummer day the Sun rises directly over the heelstone ... but that's the simple bit ...

The oldest parts of the structure, dating back to 3000 BC, demonstrate an exact understanding of Moon-rise and Moon-set. According to Gerald Hawkins and astronomer Fred Hoyle, Stonehenge also works as an **eclipse calculator**, through the use of markers moved around the 56 Aubrey Holes.

This is weird, because to predict eclipses requires a sophisticated knowledge of the 18.6-year cycle of the **Lunar Nodes**. But why would the Flintstones bother? Most eclipses just aren't visible, anyway. So this must go beyond astronomy.

Definition: Lunar Nodes – the intersections of the Moon's orbit through the Earth-Sun orbital plane, the ecliptic.

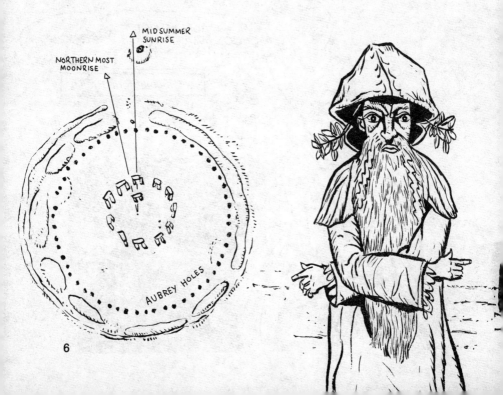

6

The Moon's nodes are called Dragon's Head and Dragon's Tail.

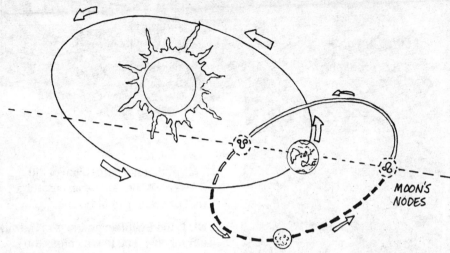

MOON'S NODES

From earliest times, the dramatic swallowing of the Sun and Moon, the lights of the sky, by a dragon or serpent has been an omen of crisis in human affairs. In modern astrology, eclipses still have the same meaning.

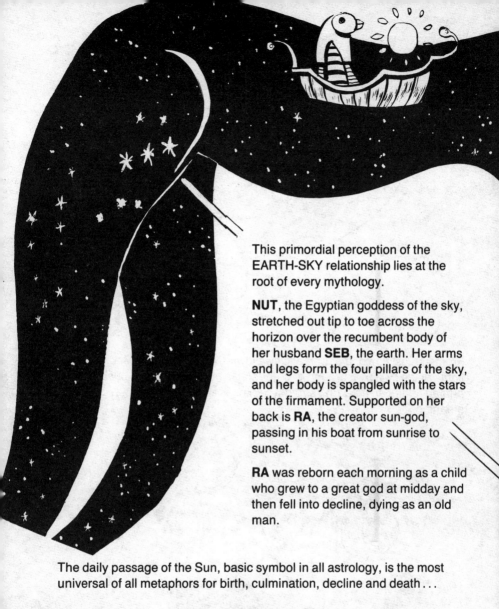

This primordial perception of the EARTH-SKY relationship lies at the root of every mythology.

NUT, the Egyptian goddess of the sky, stretched out tip to toe across the horizon over the recumbent body of her husband **SEB**, the earth. Her arms and legs form the four pillars of the sky, and her body is spangled with the stars of the firmament. Supported on her back is **RA**, the creator sun-god, passing in his boat from sunrise to sunset.

RA was reborn each morning as a child who grew to a great god at midday and then fell into decline, dying as an old man.

The daily passage of the Sun, basic symbol in all astrology, is the most universal of all metaphors for birth, culmination, decline and death . . .

ACHIEVEMENT/AUTHORITY
noon

COMING-TO-BE   **PASSING AWAY**
sunrise   sunset

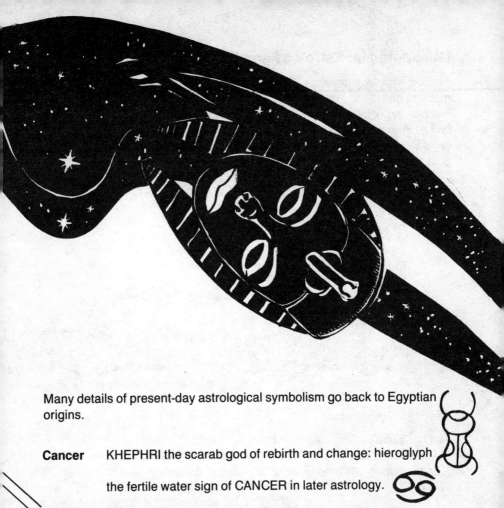

Many details of present-day astrological symbolism go back to Egyptian origins.

Cancer   KHEPHRI the scarab god of rebirth and change: hieroglyph

the fertile water sign of CANCER in later astrology.

The scarab is the dung-beetle which appears every year after the subsiding of the Nile floods, a sign that the crops will come again.

The Great Pyramids (c. 2500 BC) are the supreme example of Egyptian star-religion. They show precise alignments to the belt of Orion (Osiris) and the star Sirius (Isis, the sister and consort of Osiris). On his death, the god-king of Egypt, the Pharoah, was ritually identified with Osiris and fertilized Isis, through an act of sexual intercourse with the stars.

Mesopotamia: Astrology and Divination

Archaic astrology developed in the context of **divination**. The primary mode of divination from the 3rd millennium BC was the reading of entrails, especially the liver taken from an animal sacrificed to a god. Livers were marked out in regions of the sky, and the augur who read sky and bird omens, the liver-reader, and the early astrologer share common methods and religious attitudes.

DIAGRAM OF A LIVER

Destiny is Negotiable

The gods can be propitiated and like the king may choose to alter the divine decree. Divination isn't a forecast of a predetermined future, but a **consultation with the gods**. It is therefore an act of religion.

DESTINY IS NEGOTIABLE!

Celestial omens were recorded on a regular basis and astronomical knowledge developed steadily in the first millennium BC.

From archaic to classical astrology

The ZODIAC of twelve 30 degree signs emerged in Babylonia (a country in Mesopotamia) around the 5th century BC. Prototypes of the **horoscope** (a diagram of the heavens for a particular time) date to the late 5th century BC.

Astrology was especially associated with the **Chaldeans** from southern Babylonia, and the term "Chaldean" became synonymous with "astrologer".

From 334BC the conquests of Alexander the Great spread Greek influence from Asia Minor and Egypt through Mesopotamia and Iran to northern India. Hellenised (Greek-influenced) Egypt became a centre of astrology, with ancient Egyptian and Babylonian star-lore reworked into the new Greek science and philosophy.

Greek astrology replaced its own descriptive names for the planets with mythological names influenced by Babylonian beliefs. Drawing on associations with the old Greek gods, it produced a distinct and self-contained planetary mythology. Later astrology uses the Latin equivalents of these Greek planetary gods.

Saturn (Greek, star of **Kronos**), slowest in motion, was associated by the Babylonians with **NINURTA**, a warrior god. He was also an overseer of fate. Popular etymology linked Kronos with Chronos, Time.

Jupiter (Greek, star of **Zeus**) is an aspect of the Babylonian god **MARDUK**, slayer of the dragon, saviour of the world, herder of stars and lord of wind and storms.

Mars (Greek, star of **Ares**) is an aspect of the Babylonian **NERGAL**, the god who slays through war and fever. One of his names means "satiated by corpses", and his red colour was associated with blood and iron.

Venus (Greek, star of **Aphrodite**) is the Babylonian **ISHTAR**, and keeps her feminine and sexy side (cf **venereal**). This goddess also brought peace, sometimes by victory in war.

Mercury (Greek, star of **Hermes**) is the Babylonian **NABU**, the herald, patron of writing and scholars, and a god of buying and selling (cf **merc**hant).

Sol/Sun and **Luna**/Moon (Greek **Helios** and **Selene**) are the Babylonian male gods **SHAMASH** and **SIN**. They are less dependent on Babylonian interpretations, but the Greeks took from Babylonian astronomy the role of the Sun as "conductor" or regulator of the planets.

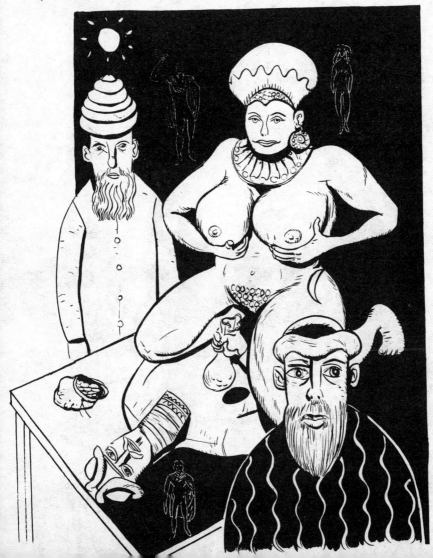

Greek-Egyptian astrology of the 3rd century BC developed the planetary sequence known as the "Chaldean order". This formed the model of the Cosmos until the time of Copernicus in the 16th century. It places planets in relative order of their apparent motion and defines their supposed distances from the earth.

Saturn (furthest from earth and slowest)

Jupiter

Mars

Sun

Venus

Mercury

Moon (nearest to earth and swiftest)

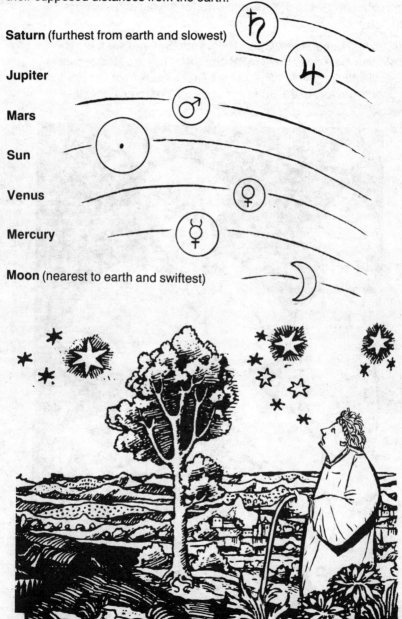

A complete system of astrological correspondences

The planets govern **TIME** itself. The seven-day week was established with each day named by a planet. Several day-names in English derive from Teutonic equivalents of the Graeco-Roman gods.

Sun - day   Sun
Mon - day   Moon
Tues - day   TIW, Mars
Wednes - day   WOTAN, Mercury
Thurs - day   THOR, Jupiter
Fri - day   FRIGG/FREYA, Venus
Satur - day   SATURN

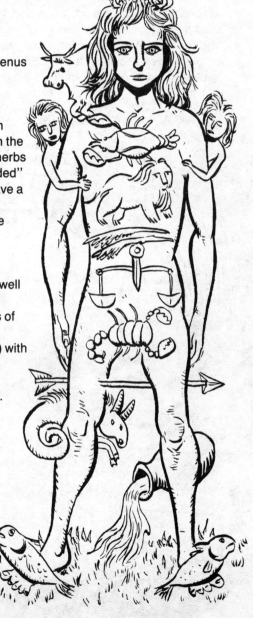

A comprehensive system of correspondences built up between planets, zodiac signs and things in the world – colours, metals, animals, herbs etc. The human body "corresponded" with the cosmos, and medicine gave a significant impetus to astrology through the melothesia, linking the signs with parts of the body:

Thus – **as above, so below**.

The Greek and Roman Stoics, as well as the Hermetic philosophers of Alexandria, all taught the oneness of the Universe, identifying the **microcosm** (the little world below) with the **macrocosm** (the great world above). Astrology is the art of interpreting this cosmic sympathy.

The Impact of Astrology on Greek Thought

The Greeks found in astrology the expression of an ordered, conscious and divine COSMOS. This is the big idea behind the greatest Greek study of astrological cosmology, Plato's **Timaeus** (c. 360 BC). It establishes the poetic and philosophical frame for all later astrology.

The **Timaeus** tells how the Demiurge, the creator-god, created the world out of the four elements – fire, earth, air and water. He gave it the most perfect form and motion, a sphere rotating on its own axis. This "world" is more than simply our earth at the centre. It is the whole visible heaven above us, the CELESTIAL SPHERE which appears to rotate around us once a day.

Everything in creation has EXISTENCE. Everything is also the SAME as something else, or DIFFERENT to it. Therefore the three basic logical categories our minds can grasp about anything and everything are Existence, Sameness and Difference.

When the Demiurge made reality (the WORLD), he gave it a soul. This is the World-Soul, and it is a compound of Sameness and Difference, mixed with Existence.

The Demiurge then split the World-Soul into two halves, creating two circular bands, laid aslant each other. These bands of soul-stuff, tilted at an angle of 23½ degrees, form the great circles of the EQUATOR and the ECLIPTIC in the Celestial Sphere. The Demiurge made them revolve.

The primary and outer band, the Equator, is single and undivided and revolves with the motion of the whole Celestial Sphere. Its motion is called the movement of the SAME.

The slanted inner band, the Ecliptic, revolves in a contrary direction and its motion is called the movement of the DIFFERENT. It is subdivided into seven unequal circles, forming the circles or spheres of the Sun, Moon and planets. The seven circles correspond in ratio to the intervals of the musical octave.

The idea of a **harmony of the spheres** in the World-Soul has entranced cosmologists down the ages.

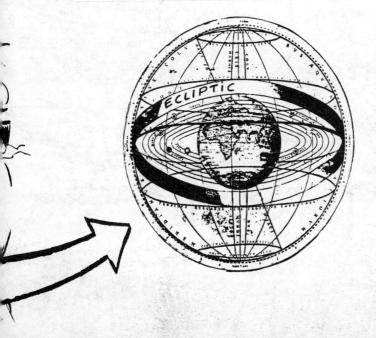

Philosophy in the Heavens

By his construction, Plato founded reason and logic in the motions of the Celestial Sphere. How does this work?

All soul-stuff throughout the World is one. When an individual employs the highest faculties of the intellect, then the motion of the individual soul is immediately united with the heavenly motions of the World-Soul. When we know the SAMENESS of things, it's because we're in touch with the Equator. When we know the DIFFERENCE between things we're really grooving the Ecliptic and the planets.

The Sowing of Souls

Having created the planetary gods, the Demiurge then took the left-over remnants of soul-stuff and divided them amongst the stars. But that's **us**! Each of us has our own particular star, and before we were incarnated in our human body we were each shown the workings of the cosmos. So contemplation of the heavens helps us recover our dim memory of what lies behind the ordinary world of our earth-bound senses.

To study the stars, then, is to study soul-stuff.

Plato's IDEAS

Later mystical astrology takes up Plato's notion of **IDEAS**, or Ideal Forms, of the things in the world around us. The signs of the zodiac especially are understood to signify the Ideas.

Aristotle (384-322 BC) is the Mr. Big of ancient philosophy. He came up with a theory that covers just about everything. He constructed a cosmic framework derived from Plato, but one which augments Plato's mysticism and provides later astrology with all it needed for a **rational and causal** explanation.

Aristotle states that the Celestial Sphere is the most perfect Being. Its rotation, initiated by the Creator, is the First Motion [*Primum Mobile*], the ultimate source of all other motion. Yet this constant, single motion cannot on its own explain the comings and goings in the world below.

PRIMUM MOBILE

I INVOKE THE MOVEMENT OF THE ECLIPTIC CIRCLE (PLATO'S DIFFERENT) AND ESPECIALLY THE SUN'S MOVEMENT ALONG THE ECLIPTIC, PRODUCING CYCLIC SEASONAL CHANGE.

ARISTOTLE

However, this still can't account for the chaos below. What happens on earth is a bit messier than these orderly heavenly changes. Things below are imperfect, and lots of changes are contingent, so chance accidents shorten or lengthen the lives of creatures.

Nevertheless, everything is still ultimately responding to the heavenly cycles.

"THE TIMES —THAT IS, THE LIVES— OF THE SEVERAL KINDS OF LIVING THINGS HAVE A NUMBER BY WHICH THEY ARE DISTINGUISHED: FOR THERE IS AN ORDER CONTROLLING ALL THINGS..."

AN ACORN SHOULD GROW INTO AN OAK TREE AND LIVE FOR HUNDREDS OF YEARS—UNLESS IT IS EATEN BY A PIG.

Fate and the Stars

If planets rule TIME and if the heavens above and the world below correspond, then it follows that planetary movements may lay out a divine plan, or pattern of Fate. Early astrologers speak of their subject as **revelation**, with contemplation of the heavens being the highest of all arts.

If we follow Aristotle, then we can't say that the heavens govern every tiny detail of life below. However, there is another strand to early astrology. The Roman Manilius [writing his poem **Astronomica** between 9 and 15 AD] typifies Stoic **fatalism** aligned with astrology.

"Fate rules the world, all things stand fixed by its immutable laws . . . it gives birth to men and at their birth determines the number of their years and the changes of their fortunes."

Judicial Astrology

So all the elements of classical astrology are now in place. Virtually nobody in ancient times doubted the direct and meaningful connection between the heavens and the world below. This perception found expression in the cosmologies of Plato and Aristotle. Greek cosmology therefore underpinned the **planetary and zodiacal correspondences**, applied to the natural and human worlds. These correspondences in turn suggest an **art of judgment** on particular destinies, known later as JUDICIAL ASTROLOGY. This employs the HOROSCOPE as its main tool.

Until the Middle Ages, astrology's cosmological foundations in Plato and Aristotle continued to give authority to the doctrine of correspondences, and to HOROSCOPY.

The major forms of judicial astrology were established by the 1st century AD. Natal astrology was the most important form, but judgments were also derived from the horoscope of conception (when known).

Another class of astrology was called **INITIATIVES** and included the following:

Inception – horoscope for the start of a venture, foundation of a city etc., to determine its prospects. This is closely linked with the idea of

Election – advance selection of the best moment to begin a venture.

Horary (interrogation) – horoscope for the moment a question is put to an astrologer, seeking advice on how to move, or a yes-no answer to the question.

Decumbiture – horoscope for the onset of illness, to provide diagnosis, critical times, and appropriate treatment.

The Greek word used for this class of astrology was **Katarche** [pronounced KA-TAR-KEY] (plural katarchai) = "initiative". This word is supercharged with an augural connotation, and suggests that katarchic astrologers viewed their practice in a divinatory and religious light. This is a **non-fated** view which allows free will through human choice.

This is the background to the definitive re-ordering of classical astrology achieved by **Ptolemy**.

Claudius Ptolemy

Claudius Ptolemy (c. 100-c. 178 AD) was an Egyptian living in Roman-ruled Alexandria, writing in Greek. Following Aristotle's groundplan, he became the architect of the medieval universe and his theory of planetary motions lasted down to Copernicus, 1400 years later.

Ptolemy's **Tetrabiblos** (the "Four Books") brings Aristotle's scientific authority into judicial astrology, and at the same time provides a rationale for the horoscopes of **conception** and **birth**.

Ptolemy's Theory

The seasonal movements of the Sun due to the earth-sun annual cycle affect the **ether**, an essence suffused through heaven and earth. This seasonal influence is represented in the differing qualities of the signs of the Zodiac.

The four elements are also affected, and through them every creature is influenced by the heavens.

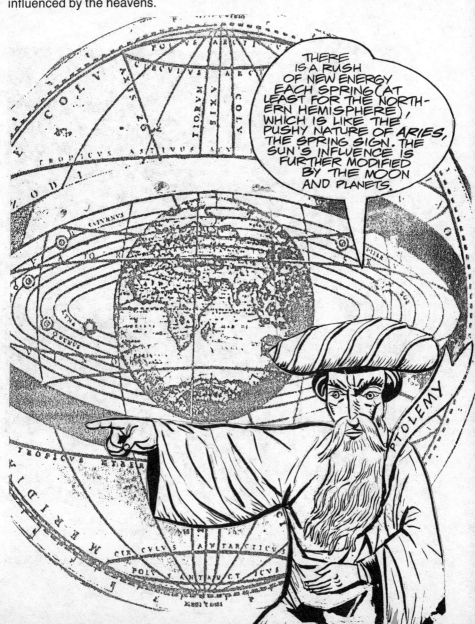

There are **two orders of astrological effect**. The first is **universal**, producing "periodic conditions" – wars, famines, pestilences, earthquakes and floods. The second is **particular** and occurs when the universal power of the heavens is indelibly impressed on a seed at its most receptive moment, the instant of fertilization or conception. As it grows, it manifests the quality of that moment, unfolding in time in relation to the planets.

Ptolemy extends this reasoning to give a naturalistic rationale for the horoscope of birth. Birth occurs in harmony with conception, so the horoscopes of conception and birth correspond.

Ptolemaic astrology only allows judgment of a particular destiny from the horoscope of a **literal** "seed-moment". This is the true beginning in time, the **causal-temporal origin**, of any creature.

But this means that the katarche (initiative) forms of horoscopy, especially horary, cannot be justified. The moment a question is asked is rarely the causal origin of the thing asked about.

From Ptolemy on, there is tension in judicial astrology between those forms which can be broadly rationalized within his Aristotelian scheme – especially natal astrology – and those which defy his logic of causal-temporal origins.

At root this is a split between astrology as DIVINATION and astrology as SCIENCE.

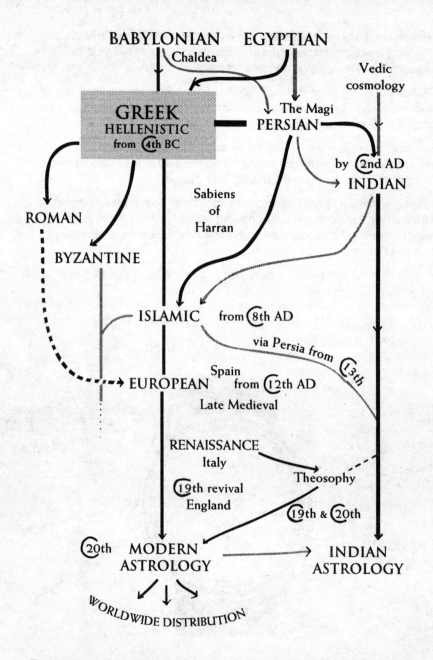

European & Indian Astrology: historical development

**"Chinese Astrology" is relatively distinct from Indo-European forms, but may share some common archaic origins.

The main structure of astrology was in place by the 3rd century AD. Let's pick up some of the themes and dilemmas that emerge in its later development.

Greek astrology is the starting point for the conservative tradition of **Indian Astrology**, flourishing in the Hindu and Buddhist cultures of India and South-East Asia. But the Indian and Islamic/European traditions diverge in how they define the **zodiac**.

The Signs of the Zodiac are twelve 30-degree segments of the ECLIPTIC circle. But where does the first Sign, Aries, start?

Because the EQUATOR and ECLIPTIC circles lie at a fixed slant to each other, there are two occasions each year when the Sun, running along the Ecliptic, gets to one of the crossing points with the Equator, around 21st March and September. Then we have an EQUINOX: day and night [= nox] are equal lengths .

The movement of the Sun from equinox to equinox is a fundamental rhythm of change through the seasons of the year. This gives a rationale for pegging the zodiac starting-point to the Northern hemisphere Spring Equinox around 21st March. Where this crossing-point at the Equator occurs is called "the First Point of Aries", and the 12 Signs are counted from it.

Precession

Here comes a headache for the early astrologers. The SIGNS originally drew their names and a good part of their symbolism from the constellations (imaginative groupings) of fixed stars which lie along the ecliptic. However, when compared with the background constellations, the Equinox point **isn't** fixed. By the phenomenon of **precession of the equinox** this point, and therefore the zodiac of 12 signs pegged to it, drifts backwards against the fixed stars at the rate of one degree in 72 years. A full cycle takes about 26,000 years.

Zodiacs Diverge

After some confusion, classical Graeco-Roman astrology settled for a zodiac measured from the Equinox point, and therefore aligned with the annual seasonal rhythm. This is called the **tropical zodiac**. Indian astrology stayed with the **sidereal zodiac**, keeping the starting point of its 12 Signs aligned with the beginning of the fixed-star constellation of Aries. Over the centuries the two zodiacs have slipped further and further out of synch. The difference between the two zodiacs is currently about 24 degrees, getting on for a whole sign of the zodiac. So if you go to an Indian astrologer as a (tropical) Sun-sign Aries, he could turn you into a (sidereal) Sun-sign Pisces!

But there is another answer which most typifies the symbolic and poetic mind-set of astrology. The 12 signs of both zodiacs are two reflections of the same **symbolic forms**. The zodiac is an imaginative assignation and because astrology is a symbol system, a choice of zodiacs is **not an either-or, right or wrong, choice**. Both therefore "show" in their own different ways.

Let's leave Indian astrology to its own history and return to the development of European astrology...

Struggles with Christianity

Christianity was an early rival pitted against astrology, and more often than not its number one enemy. Perhaps they are both competing for the Soul and Destiny.

St. Augustine (354-430) is the heavyweight Christian critic. His knock-out punches come from being well versed in astrology, since he studied it before his conversion to Christianity. He employs both rational-scientific and spiritual arguments.

He also accuses astrologers of slippery logic by attempting to justify astrology sometimes as **causes** and other times as **signs**. He then clobbers them on either count. How?

Determinism...or Devil's Work?

However, when astrologers make successful predictions, they are aided by **demons**.

The aim of the demons is to seduce the soul into giving up its free will by accepting determinism. In this way demons **subjugate the soul** to the pagan deities of the stars. "Astrology is congress with demons" or "the work of the Devil", which is the line taken by modern-day fundamentalists and the Vatican alike.

The Star of Bethlehem

The Star of Bethlehem and the story of the three Magi (Persian astrologer-priests) poses a dilemma for Christian opponents of astrology.

Many medieval astrologers, following a rationalised Aristotelian concept of the Cosmos, accepted the view that the star was a super-natural sign.

However, Johannes Kepler's hypothesis (circa 1600) has been affirmed by modern scholarship. The "star" was a conjunction of Jupiter and Saturn.

This symbolism ties in with the prophecies of that era concerning a messiah amongst the Jews.

1. The conjunctions occurred at the end of Pisces, ruled by Jupiter
2. Jupiter is the planet of kings
3. and Saturn rules the Jews ... hence, **king of the Jews**.

Three conjunctions = three kings.

One Christian argument allows the astrology but re-takes the story in an attempt to kill it off. Tertullian (c. 200 AD) believes that gold, frankincense and myrrh symbolize pagan magic and astrology.

But Tertullian's logic could get him into trouble. For the Christian, Christ is reborn in **every** child. Just as the Magi were permitted by God to interpret the signs showing the destiny of Christ, on that account the great mission for astrology is likewise to offer its gifts to **every** nativity.

As Christianity gained hold in the Roman world, astrology was treated as a heretical remnant of paganism. It virtually disappeared in "the Dark Ages" in Europe after the western Empire disintegrated (Rome sacked by the Visigoths in 410).

In the Greek-speaking former Eastern Roman Empire (the Byzantime Empire) . . .

. . . In the West, Latin was the educated language, but the survival of classical learning depended mainly on the monasteries. Although **judicial astrology** died off, astrological correspondences remained in common use, especially the zodiac symbolism which expresses time and the seasons.

The momentum now switches to Persian, Arabic and Jewish astrologers who came together in the Islamic civilization which arose in the three centuries after the death of Mohammed (632 AD).

Islamic culture assimilated Greek philosophy, medicine, and science, with Aristotle having primary status. Many Greek texts lost to the Latin West were translated into Arabic, including astrology.

Major figures developed the Greek basics into astronomically sophisticated forms which still underpin astrology today, eg ·

Al-Kindi (died c. 870 AD), called the "philosopher of the Arabs", translated Aristotle into Arabic, but was also influenced by Hermetism.

His student Abu-Ma'shar (787-886 AD) and Masha'allah, a Jewish astrologer (8th century AD). We find their names and aphorisms quoted endlessly in later European astrology.

The Medieval revival in Europe

Europe had to re-learn astrology from the Arabs. From the 12th century, Arabic scientific texts were translated into Latin, including lost Greek works. Astrology came too; Ptolemy's **Tetrabiblos** was translated in 1138.

Ptolemy's cosmology and the **Aristotelian rationale** for astrology allowed a compromise with Christianity and secured its place in the medieval universities.

St. Thomas Aquinas (c. 1225-74) accepted judicial astrology at the level of bodily influence. Since the soul can rise above the flesh, it can rise above planetary influence.

With a narrow view of astrology as horoscopes and predictions, it's difficult to see the **big picture** of the celestial metaphor of macrocosm-microcosm. This symbolism is all-pervading in medieval science, medicine and art.

Dante's **Divine Comedy** (c. 1307) is a supreme example. His vision is expressed in the Platonic symbolism of Equator, Ecliptic and the Equinox. He weaves actual observed phenomena of the planets in Spring 1301 into his vision. His planetary heavens are developed from conventional astrological symbolism. He quotes the Aquinas line which permits horoscopes. To cap it all he attributes his own poetic genius to the influence of his birth sign, Gemini!

> . . . I saw I was in the Heaven of the Twain. *
>
> O stars of glory, from whose light on high
> A mighty virtue poureth forth, to you
> I owe such genius as doth in me lie
>
> * Gemini, the Twins
>
> from **Paradiso**, Canto XXI

On the other hand, Dante was tough on **predictive** astrologers. Guido Bonatti (= Bonatus, 13th century), a founding father of European judicial astrology, turns up in Hell. He is with the sorcerers, and like them his head is turned back to front as punishment for trying to see into the future.

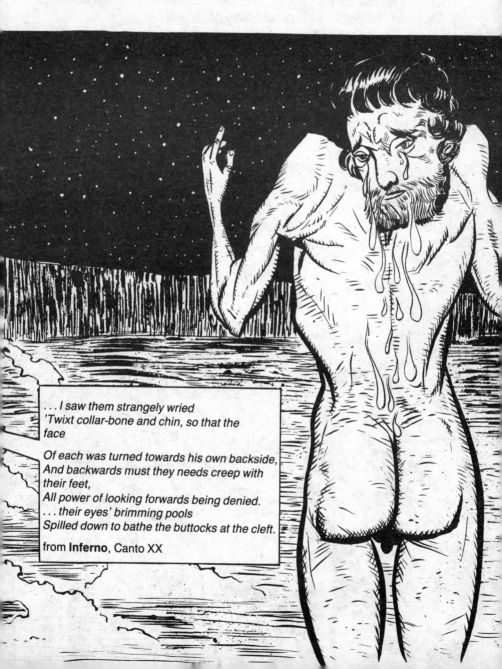

... I saw them strangely wried
'Twixt collar-bone and chin, so that the face

Of each was turned towards his own backside,
And backwards must they needs creep with their feet,
All power of looking forwards being denied.
... their eyes' brimming pools
Spilled down to bathe the buttocks at the cleft.

from **Inferno**, Canto XX

Renaissance Magic & Astrology

The Renaissance started in Italy as a cultural re-birth inspired by pagan antiquity, especially that of Greece. Christianity was reinterpreted as the culmination of a **mystery** tradition going back to the mythical Hermes Trismegistos (thrice-greatest Hermes). The Hermetic axiom is "As above, so below" – big-picture astrology again!

The leading Renaissance philosopher Marsilio Ficino (1433-1499) taught medical astrology and developed astrological music therapy – the old "harmony of the spheres".

Ficino combined astrology with **natural magic**.

Ficino also practised stronger magic, invoking planetary Intelligences through talismans and ritual.

Ficino's approach to horoscope judgment moved to a free-will **katarchic** form (see p23). For him, astrology works like the omens of augury, not like science. It is "poetic metaphor, not reason or logic".

This leads to a crunch! Ficino mocked contemporary astrologers of Florence.

Ficino's pupil, Pico della Mirandola, took this up in his **Disputations against Divinatory Astrology** (1495). With its armoury of rational and scientific arguments, this supplied firepower for attacks on astrology for at least 200 years.

The Renaissance magicians condemned astrologers who over-rode the free choice of the soul. But this clash also signals that mainstream judicial astrology (hijacking Aristotle) isn't a straight subset of European occultism (tuned into Plato). These two tend to run on separate tracks.

As with its use in magic, astrology provides a symbolic framework for supernatural inspiration. **Nostradamus** (1503-1566) observed the 20-year cycle of Jupiter-Saturn conjunctions, like the Arab astrologers before him, to prefigure the epochs of history and trigger his prophetic function.

At a more comprehensible level, the Renaissance brought a flowering of sophisticated horoscopy, with many instances of influence on princes and Popes.

John Dee elected the Coronation of Elizabeth Ist. He found her an unusual day (15 January 1559) when the Sun and the "benefics", Venus and Jupiter, were inter-aspecting favourably the very same planets in Elizabeth's birth-chart (7 Sept 1533). It's a nifty piece of craft, and good Queen Bess **did** hold England together for 44 years!

Johannes Kepler (1571-1630) is a scientific hero for his development of the modern theory of planetary orbits, but he was also a mystical astrologer through and through, dedicated to proving the "harmony of the spheres".

He condemned the irrationality of conventional astrology, but sought to **reform** horoscopy, not to destroy it. He reminded astrology's critics "not to throw the baby out with the bathwater".

NOTHING EXISTS AND NOTHING HAPPENS IN THE VISIBLE HEAVENS THAT IS NOT ECHOED IN SOME HIDDEN MANNER BY THE FACULTIES OF EARTH AND NATURE: THE FACULTIES OF THE SPIRIT OF THIS WORLD (ANIMA MUNDI) ARE AFFECTED IN THE SAME MEASURE AS HEAVEN ITSELF.

Times were changing fast. The 17th century saw European astrology's last flowering, but also ushered in its catastrophic decline.

Two notable astrologers epitomize competing themes of astrology's tradition.

Morin de Villefranche (1583-1659) reformed horoscopy along **classical Aristotelian/Ptolemaic** lines, geared to exact prediction. He rejected horary as irrational. His high-Latin opus, **Astrologia Gallica**, disappeared into oblivion.

The approach of William Lilly (1602-1681) is **katarchic and magical** and he was a master of mundane astrology (political and social) and horary.

He gained fame through predictions in the English Civil War.

In a style reminiscent of Nostradamus, Lilly employed a mysterious "prophetical astrology". His best-known feat concerns his "hieroglyphic" predictions of the Great Plague of London (1665) and the Fire of London (1666). *

In his textbook **Christian Astrology** (1647), he demonstrates that an exact predictive astrology nevertheless allows free will and is compatible with Christianity. His beautifully crafted judgments coupled with pithy interpretations secured the survival of an effective method of **horary astrology** into present times.

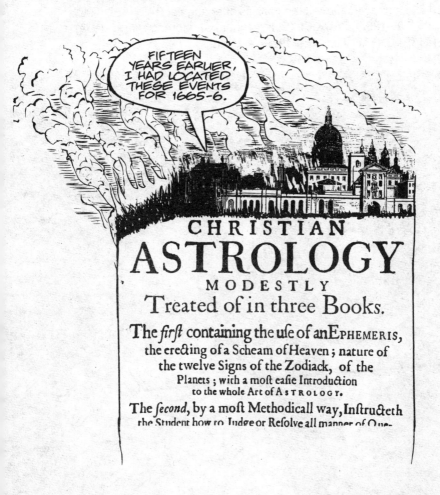

* Because of this he was summoned before the Parliamentary Committee investigating the fire, in case he had started it to prove his astrology.

Decline and Rise

The "Age of Enlightenment" after 1700 saw European astrology simply drop away for the intellectual élite. It retreated to a baseline in folklore and popular almanacs. Horoscopy virtually finished as an effective practice – except in England with a tiny band of eccentrics.

Astrology picked itself up off the floor in early 19th-century England. Astrologers often adapted metaphors drawn from science, such as electricity and magnetism, but the romantic reaction to rationalism also led to the Victorian delight in the occult. This helps to explain why leading astrologers named themselves after angels. RAPHAEL (R.C. Smith 1795-1832), ZADKIEL (Commander R.J. Morrison (1795-1874), SEPHARIAL (W.R. Old 1864-1929), and others.

Theosophy

Helena Petrova Blavatsky (1831-1891) founded the Theosophical Society in 1875. Theosophy's "secret doctrine" underlying all religions, with its concepts of karma and reincarnation, provided the missing spiritual link for many astrologers.

Alan Leo (W.F. Allen 1860-1917), an indefatigable organizer and writer, brings the story of astrology into the 20th century.

Inspired by Theosophy, he revamped natal astrology away from the tough-minded predictive legacy of its tradition, and brought it into line with the more psychological concern of the modern age. From that point on, modern astrology has never looked back . . .

PART II – ASTROLOGY PRIMER

Since the beginning of its 20th century revival, astrology in the West has grown stronger, despite intellectual and academic hostility. The starsign columns have given it a popular form, but the more complex practice of individual horoscope interpretation has also flourished.

Astrology is a universal language of the imagination, shared by humanity over the millennia. The Babylonian on his ziggurat, the Greek at Delphi, the Renaissance magician and today's stargazer on Brooklyn Bridge would all share a significant common understanding if they saw an eclipse at noon or sexy Venus joining Mars.

Modern astrology has kept the fundamental structure of traditional astrology. This primer will help you to speak its language by giving you keys to the basic vocabulary.

The Solar System

The Earth and planets orbit around the Sun, moving in the same direction but taking different lengths of time. The Moon orbits around the Earth. All the orbits are roughly on the same plane, so the whole "Solar System" is like a flat dish.

SUN, MOON, MERCURY, VENUS, MARS, JUPITER, SATURN, URANUS, NEPTUNE, PLUTO

Note that the diagram is not drawn to scale. Properly speaking, the band of the Zodiac should be imagined on the vastly distant CELESTIAL SPHERE, in the realm of the fixed stars.

Seen from the Earth ⊕, the different distances of the Sun, Moon and other planets from the Earth are of no account. All appear equally "projected" against the band of the Zodiac.

In the above diagram, a line of sight from the Earth through the Sun projects the Sun into the last degrees of Cancer(♋). Hence the Sun is "in" ♋. Similarly the Moon is here "in" ♏.

Retrogradation: from the Earth, planets (but never ☉ & ☽) appear to move backwards (retrograde ℞) for certain periods. This will happen when a planet is on the same side of the solar system as the Earth (in diagram, ♆ is ℞).

LOGIC OF THE ZODIAC

The twelve signs of the Zodiac group into three MODES and four ELEMENTS.

	Cardinal	**Fixed**	**Mutable**
FIRE	Aries	Leo	Sagittarius
EARTH	Capricorn	Taurus	Virgo
AIR	Libra	Aquarius	Gemini
WATER	Cancer	Scorpio	Pisces

The **MODES** are three different ways of action or phases of manifestation:

CARDINAL INITIATING – Doing, turning points, action.
When the Sun enters these signs it inaugurates each of the four seasons.

FIXED   MAINTAINING – Endurance, stability.
As the Sun travels through these signs, each season comes to its height.

MUTABLE MOVING ON – Adapting, disseminating.
When the Sun is in these signs, each season is in transition.

ELEMENTS

Fire and Air are POSITIVE, rising upwards, extrovert. Earth and Water are NEGATIVE, moving downwards, introvert.

The meaning of the elements comes from how we experience them.

FIRE Fire is the light which brings into view. It is heat and warmth and it animates us. It is untouchable, divine – and dangerous. It expresses as assertion, self-confidence, love of life.

EARTH We stand on earth, it grounds us and supports us. It is matter, the substance of anything. It expresses as dependability, materialism and common sense.

AIR Air is spacious and abstract, like the sky between heaven and earth. It interpenetrates things and carries breath, words, thoughts. It expresses as humanity, language and intelligence.

WATER Water flows and finds its own level. It cleanses, dissolves and fertilises. It expresses as emotion, imagination and empathy.

The Humours

The humours of medieval science and medicine, Aristotle's four principles of HOT, COLD, MOIST & DRY, and the astrological elements, are all connected.

HOT & DRY   = FIRE (Choleric temperament)
COLD & DRY   = EARTH (Melancholic temperament)
HOT & MOIST   = AIR (Sanguine temperament)
COLD & MOIST = WATER (Phlegmatic temperament)

Some modern astrologers correlate the elements with the psychological types of **Carl Jung**.

Fire – Intuition   Earth – Sensation
Air – Intellect   Water – Feeling

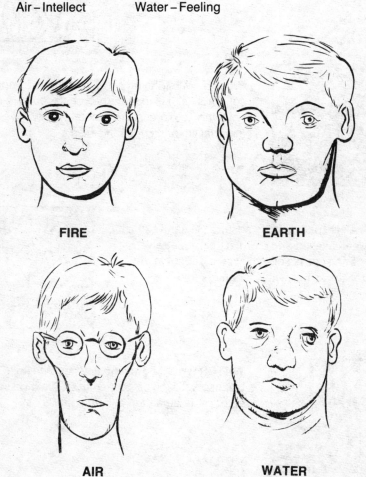

FIRE   EARTH

AIR   WATER

THE COSMIC BEING & SIGNS OF THE ZODIAC

The order of the signs shows the body and the life cycle of the "Cosmic Being". This gives another line on the symbolism and psychology of the Zodiac.

ARIES THE RAM Positive, ruled by Mars. The head. Cardinal fire (the spark, intense flame).

This is the first sign and the cosmic being comes into the world head first. Aries is innocent and immediate, moves off self-interest and **does** things. Pioneering, active and head-strong.

Key phrase:

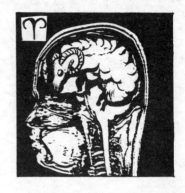

I AM (ME FIRST)!

TAURUS THE BULL Negative, ruled by Venus. Throat and neck. Fixed earth (field and forest).

The 2nd sign shows embodiment and physical necessity. Taurus values material security. Possessive, building and conserving.

Key phrase:

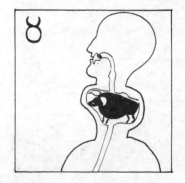

I OWN.

GEMINI THE TWINS Positive, Mercury. Arms and hands. Mutable air (breezes).

The 3rd sign, and Cosmic Being gets curious. Gemini connects, communicates, networks. Quick, ingenious, but divisive.

Key phrase:

I SPEAK.

CANCER THE CRAB Negative, ruled by the Moon. Breast and stomach. Cardinal water (the sea).

The 4th sign creates a home and emotional security. Maternal, nourishing, protective and defensive.

Key phrase:

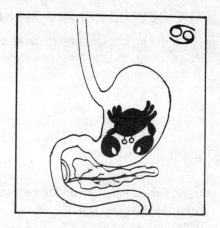

LEO THE LION Positive, ruled by the Sun. Heart and back. Fixed fire (the blaze).

The 5th sign, the Cosmic Being gets creative! Leo is self-expressive, egotistical, centre stage. Courageous, proud and loyal.

Key phrase:

VIRGO THE VIRGIN Negative, ruled by Mercury. The digestive system. Mutable earth (field and harvest).

The 6th sign, and Virgo adapts to the environment with skills and crafts. Service, analysis, discrimination and perfection.

Key phrase:

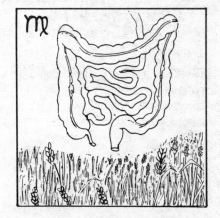

LIBRA THE SCALES Positive, ruled by Venus. Kidneys, lower back. Cardinal air (the wind).

The 7th sign shows the half-way stage when Cosmic Being encounters "otherness" and balances subject and object. Relating, harmonizing and intellectual.

Key phrase:

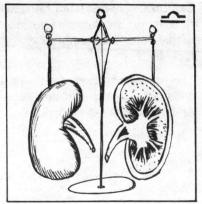

SCORPIO THE SCORPION Negative, ruled by Mars and Pluto. Genitals and excretory system. Fixed water (the tarn and dam).

The 8th sign brings sexuality, power, magic and the mysteries of life and death. Penetrating, transforming and avenging.

Key phrase:

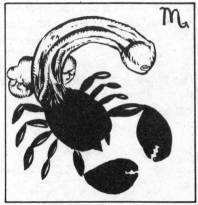

SAGITTARIUS THE ARCHER Positive, ruled by Jupiter. Hips and thighs. Mutable fire (the dancing flame).
In the 9th sign, Cosmic Being travels, explores and targets things. The search for meaning and freedom. Visionary and optimistic.

Key phrase:

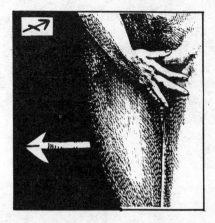

CAPRICORN THE GOAT Negative, ruled by Saturn. Bones, teeth and skeleton. Cardinal earth (rocks and mountains).

The 10th sign consolidates the past, creates and controls boundaries. Ambitious, political, responsible.

Key phrase:

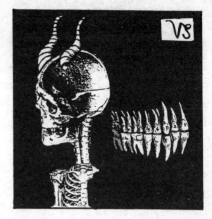

AQUARIUS THE WATER CARRIER Positive, ruled by Saturn and Uranus. Shins, ankles and circulation. Fixed air (the sky).

The 11th sign shows friendship, group life and shared ideology. The laws of thought and the principle of things. Reforming and humane.

Key phrase:

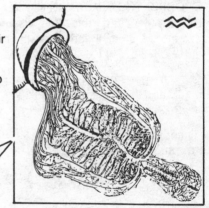

PISCES THE FISH Negative, ruled by Jupiter and Neptune. Feet. Mutable water (the stream).

The last sign, and Cosmic Being prepares for the end. Renunciation of personal desire for the good of the whole. Redemption, compassion, charity.

Key phrase:

(The fishes, symbol of Christ)

THE PLANETS

The word "planet" means "wanderer". Unlike fixed stars in the constellations, planets "wander" against the Zodiac band. In addition to the seven traditional planets, three Outer Planets beyond Saturn – trans-Saturnians – are visible by telescope – Uranus, Neptune and Pluto.

Planetary Glyphs

The planetary glyphs slowly evolved up to the Renaissance period. Three principles – spirit, soul and matter – combine in varied ways to reflect each planet's meaning.

The circle of **Spirit**   ◯
The cross of **Matter**   ✚
The crescent of **Soul** or **Psyche**, mediating spirit and matter   ☽

Saturn ♄ is matter above soul, the soul imprisoned and embodied.

Jupiter ♃ is soul above matter, the imaginative power of psyche to rise above such bondage.

Venus ♀ and **Mars** ♂ (older version ♂) also pair.

Magical **Mercury** ☿ combines all three.

Outer Planet glyphs appear to share this pattern.

Uranus ♅ is two soul-crescents, split apart by matter.

Neptune ♆ is soul, struck through by matter (sacrifice).

Pluto ♇ combines all three (sometimes drawn ♇).

Sun-Sign Dates

The Sun enters each sign on or around these dates:

ARIES	21 March	Spring Equinox
TAURUS	21 April	
GEMINI	21 May	
CANCER	21 June	Summer Solstice
LEO	23 July	
VIRGO	23 August	
LIBRA	22 September	Autumn Equinox
SCORPIO	22 October	
SAGITTARIUS	22 November	
CAPRICORN	22 December	Winter Solstice
AQUARIUS	21 January	
PISCES	18 February	

THE SUN

The Sun rules the sign Leo and the Day. It is the **centre** of the planetary system, the **source** of **light** and life. Creative and constant, it regulates nature through the seasons. It is Being, spirit, heart, the essence of things, consciousness and supremacy. It is male, Father, King.

Solar individuals shine, their nature is heroic, noble, purposive, loyal and generous. They are centre-stage, the star and leader. Negatively it is arrogant and disdainful. Psychologically, it is self-identity and the ego. In Jung's terms, it is the **individuation process**.

Other associations:

colours	– orange-yellow and scarlet
plants	– heliotropes, sunflower, marigold, dandelion ("tooth of the lion")
animals	– royal (swan), heralding the sun (cockerel)
occupations	– kings, directors, organizers, performers
places	– palaces, theatres

THE MOON

The Moon rules Cancer and the Night. It orbits the earth, waxing and waning to create the monthly cycle and pull the tides. It is receptive and changeable, a mirror reflecting solar light. It is instinct, soul, the flux and rhythm of nature, the unconscious, mysterious and occult. To follow the Moon is to "go with the flow". It is the Roman goddess Diana, protector of women and childbirth.

Lunar individuals reflect, their nature is shy, tender, protective, imaginative and psychic. Negative qualities are timidity, over-sensitivity and "lunacy". Psychologically, the Moon is the personal unconscious, habitual responses, patterns established in childhood, basic needs and instincts.

Other associations:

colours	– white and silver
plants	– round, watery fruits (melon), thick, juicy leaves (cabbage)
animals	– creatures of night or water – owl, snail, frog
occupations	– cleaners, brewers, midwives, sailors
places	– sea, shore-line, harbour

MERCURY

Mercury rules Gemini and Virgo. It is the fast moving planet closest to the Sun and the wing-footed Greek messenger god (HERMES). It is intellect, language, communication, trade and theft. It is the magician, crossing boundaries between male and female (**herma**phrodite), conscious and unconscious, mind and matter, life and death (the soul's guide into the underworld).

Mercurial individuals are quick-witted, skilled, ingenious and learned. Negatively, it is crafty, verbose and amoral. Psychologically, it is the trickster nature of the psyche, revealed through slips of the tongue and Freud's "talking cure".

Other associations:

colours	– stripes, mottles, mixed
plants	– beans, walnuts, flowers without a smell
animals	– cunning, mischievous, chattering (monkey, parrot)
occupations	– the media, merchants, clerks, accountants, scholars
places	– shops, schools, stations

VENUS

Venus rules Libra and Taurus. It is the star of lovers, the Greek goddess APHRODITE, erotic, desirable and pleasurable. Inspirational and joyous, it is beauty, peace, victory in war, laughter, friendship and the arts.

Venusian individuals relate to others and seek partnership. They are sociable, tolerant, compromising, lovers of beauty, art, wealth and luxury. Negative qualities are lewdness, promiscuity and over-indulgence. Psychologically, it is evaluation, self-worth, and the desire for completion through the significant Other.

Other associations:

colours	– white, green
plants	– scented (rose, daffodil), smooth-leafed (lilly), sweet (fig, apple, peach, plum)
animals	– gentle, friendly (dove, dolphin)
occupations	– fashion and beauty, art, diplomacy
places	– bedrooms, gardens

MARS

Mars rules Aries and Scorpio. It is the red planet of force, will, action, physical energy and sexual desire. It is the Greek god of battle (ARES), angry, quarrelsome and complaining.

Martian individuals are aggressive, penetrating and defiant, singular and uncompromising. They are champions of life and death. Negatively, it is a malcontent, violent and irrationally destructive. Psychologically it is libido, psychic energy as a whole, the power of self-assertion and the ability to separate.

Other associations:

colours	– red or orange
plants	– sharp, stinging or bitter, ginger, pepper, nettles
animals	– predators – wolf, shark
occupations	– soldiers, surgeons, athletes
places	– furnaces, foundries, slaughter-houses

JUPITER

Jupiter rules Sagittarius and Pisces. It is the largest of the traditional planets, the Greek ZEUS, king of the gods and thunderous lord of the sky. It is the law-maker, beneficent and protective, creating opportunity, growth and progress. It is providence, good fortune, faith, hope and charity.

Jupiterian individuals are magnanimous, noble, optimistic, liberal and freedom-loving. They guide and cheer others, offering wise counsel. Negatively, it is excessive, domineering, hypocritical and arrogant. Psychologically it is the search for meaning, the experience of the numinous and the desire for soul-growth.

Other associations:

colours	– purple, blue, sea-green
plants	– rapid growth like privet, far-spreading like vines
animals	– large and powerful – horse, elephant, whale, eagle
occupations	– lawyers, priests, counsellors, developers, empire – builders, actors, clowns
places	– open spaces, public places, plains, panoramic views

SATURN

Saturn rules Aquarius and Capricorn. It is the most distant and slow-moving of the visible planets, associated with the Greek god CHRONOS. It rules fate and time, the past, limits and boundaries, form, structure and the skeleton. It is cold, old, controlled and conservative.

Saturnine individuals are serious, ambitious, orthodox and self-disciplined. Negatively, it is melancholic and solitary, showing envy, suffering, fear and guilt. Psychologically, it is the repressed material of the "shadow", the disowned and inferior side of an individual, manifesting as scape-goating.

Other associations:

plants	– poisonous or deep-rooted. Yew, hemlock, comfrey, nightshade
colours	– black, olive
animals	– vermin and lice
occupations	– politicians, scientists, architects
places	– mountains, desolate places, mines

URANUS

Uranus, co-ruler of Aquarius, is the first new planet beyond Saturn, and its discovery in 1781 wiped out the medieval cosmos. It is the Greek sky god, OURANOS, castrated by Chronos (= Saturn). It liberates by destroying Saturn's tradition and authority. It is the Scientific Enlightenment and shows Intellect exalted above Nature.

The Uranian individual is a wilful outsider, a reformer, humanist and eccentric genius. Negatively, Uranus is anarchy, tyranny and inhumanity. Psychologically, it shows dissociation, resistance and the castration complex.

Other Associations

Historical events coinciding with Uranus' discovery show its revolutionary nature – French Revolution (1789), American War of Independence (1781). Its scientific nature is revealed in electricity (Galvani 1780) and inventions of the Industrial Revolution. Occupations include technology, electronics and aeronautics.

NEPTUNE

Neptune, discovered in 1846, is the second of the new planets beyond Saturn. Greek god of the sea (POSEIDON), it merges things into a limitless and nebulous state. It represents idealization, sacrifice and an unconscious, collective identity. It is fantasy, paranormal experience, psycho-physical reality and the desire for the "beyond" in all its forms, whether through mysticism or drugs.

Neptunian individuals may be artists, visionaries or martyrs. Negatively, it is deceptive and deluded. Psychologically it shows hysteria, projection and the transference.

Other Associations

Historical events coinciding with Neptune's discovery show its impersonal and collective nature – Darwin's theory of evolution (1846), the Communist Manifesto (1848) and the rise of socialism. Its other-worldly dimension shows in modern spiritualism (Fox Sisters 1847), anaesthetics and hypnosis. Occupations include film, advertising, and the petro-chemical and pharmaceutical industries.

PLUTO

Pluto, discovered in 1930, is the Greek HADES, lord of the underworld, keeper of the dead. He wears the helmet of invisibility and rarely visits the upper world, but when he does it is to transform by annihilating outmoded forms. Pluto shows the cycle of birth-death-rebirth. By a secondary association with the Roman god PLUTUS, it represents the vast sources of power and wealth hidden under the earth.

A Plutonic individual is a lone wolf, concerned with power and possessed of an unusual, transforming gift. Negatively, it shows as sociopathic behaviour, rape and violation or as non-entity. Psychologically it is psychosis, obsession, and also Thanatos, the death instinct.

Other associations

Historical events around Pluto's discovery include the splitting of the atom, Fascism and Stalinism, the rise of Big Brother, international terrorism and organized crime (Mafia). It also shows as nihilism and surrealism (Magritte).

METAL-PLANET AFFINITIES

Traditional astrology's association of each planet with a metal forms the basis of alchemy. Modern knowledge has also brought curious connections to light.

The Chaldean Order of the planets corresponds with a scaling of the metals, based on four key physical properties which define a metal:

– lustre
– resonance
– malleability
– conductivity

The Moon, the nearest planet, has the highest of each property. Saturn, the furthest planet, has the lowest, as follows: [scaled to silver as 100]

Planet: Chaldean Order	Metal	Thermal Conductivity	Electrical Conductivity
MOON	Silver	100	100
MERCURY	Quicksilver	(Not scaled – usually liquid)	
VENUS	Copper	94	95
SUN	Gold	74	72
MARS	Iron	20	17
JUPITER	Tin	16	13
SATURN	Lead	8	8

"We see that the planetary movement is metamorphosed into the properties of earthly metals."
– Rudolph Hauschka

A few of the many metal-planet affinities are as follows:

MOON   Reflects the light of the Sun.
Silver is used in backing mirrors and light-sensitive film.

MERCURY   Quicksilver/Mercury. Gives a speedy response through
thermometers and forms amalgams with other metals
(dental fillings).

VENUS   Malleable copper is used for IUDs in the service of
Aphrodite, and for healing, copper bracelets.

SUN   Incorruptible gold is the most desired of metals, the
wedding ring and the gold standard.

MARS   Hard iron is for weapons, vehicles and steel.

JUPITER   Just a hint of preserving power in the tin can!

SATURN   Dull, heavy lead, a poor conductor. Insulates and isolates,
blocking electricity and radiation – lead apron for X Ray
protection.

A Black Alchemy

Uranium, like Uranus itself, is on the edge of visibility. Elements heavier
than lead are unstable, existing naturally only in small quantities.
Abhorrent to nature, they break down in radioactive decay.

PLANETARY DIGNITY AND DEBILITY

The relationship of planets with signs is founded in a traditional system known as the **Dignities and Debilities** of the planets. Many of its nuances have faded from modern natal astrology, but two important pairings are still in use, **Rulership and Detriment**, **Exaltation and Fall**.

Rulerships: Each planet rules one or two signs, following a pattern based on the division of the Zodiac into a solar half (Leo to Capricorn) and a lunar half (Cancer to Aquarius). The Sun and Moon rule Leo and Cancer. Reflecting the Chaldean Order, each remaining planet rules two signs, showing two sides of its nature in a positive/day sign and a negative/night sign, fanning out either side of Cancer and Leo in each half of the Zodiac, as follows:

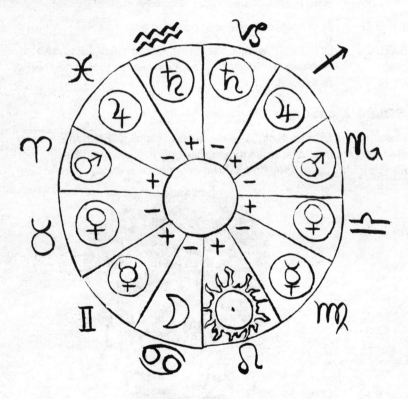

Co-rulerships: The modern planets subvert the traditional scheme, but the following **co-rulerships** are commonly accepted: Uranus co-rules Aquarius, Neptune co-rules Pisces, Pluto co-rules Scorpio.

The planetary rulerships also make **symbolic sense**. Planets rule signs because they have an affinity with them and are strengthened by the signs. The positive or negative dimension of the sign brings out the planet's nature in differing ways. For example, Jupiter's expansive nature accords with both the exploring side of Sagittarius (positive) and the charitable side of Pisces (negative). Similarly, Mars is a hot-headed soldier in Aries (positive), but a secret agent in Scorpio (negative).

Detriment

Planets are in **detriment**, or out of tune, in the signs opposite to those which they rule. For example, co-operative Venus is spoiled by aggressive Aries and revengeful Scorpio.

Exaltation & Fall

Planets in certain signs are **exalted** and gain in strength. Planets opposite to their signs of exaltation are in **fall**, pulled down in power and weakened.

Planet	Exaltation	Fall
SUN	Aries	Libra
MOON	Taurus	Scorpio
MERCURY	Virgo	Pisces
VENUS	Pisces	Virgo
MARS	Capricorn	Cancer
JUPITER	Cancer	Capricorn
SATURN	Libra	Aries

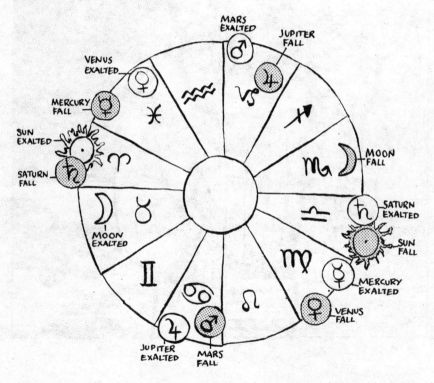

What's the symbolic logic here? Mars is exalted in Capricorn because the force of Mars is disciplined and directed, like an army. Yet Mars in fall in Cancer is defensive and sensitive and has no stomach for a fight. Pisces exalts Venus by giving boundless sympathy, Virgo pulls her down by critical analysis. Can you work out some of the others?

ASPECTS

Aspects are divisions of the 360 degree circle, the angle between any two planets or factors, measured in arcs of zodiacal longitude, from the earth centre.

The Conjunction (0 degrees) shows a uniting of the planets and the Opposition (division by 2) shows them resisting each other. Division by 3 (and 6 or 12) gives **easy, harmonious** ("good") aspects. Division by 4 (and 8) produces **hard, difficult** ("bad") aspects.

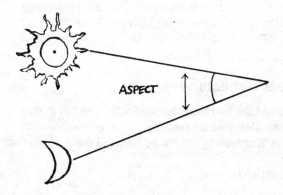

Orbs: The orb is the number of degrees allowed on either side of the exact aspect for the aspect still to operate. Older astrologers varied the orbs depending on the planets involved, but modern astrology has standardized orbs for each aspect.

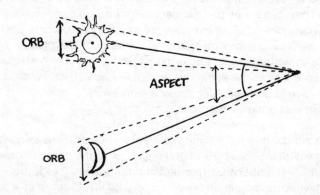

SYMBOL	o	NAME	ORB	MEANING
		The Major Aspects (Ptolemaic)		
☌	0	Conjunction	8	Identity, unity
☍	180	Opposition	8	Challenge, conflict
△	120	Trine	8	Harmony, co-operation
□	90	Square	8	Struggle, crisis
✳	60	Sextile	6 or 4	Creativity
		The Minor Aspects		
∟	45	Semi-square	2	Stressful
⬐	135	Sesquiquadrate	2	Stressful
⚺	30	Semi-sextile	2	Helpful
⚻	150	Quincunx	2	Stressful (health)

Dissociate Aspects

Remember to look for **dissociate** aspects, when planets in orb cross over different elements and modes. For example, Mercury at 27 Capricorn is in conjunction with the Sun at 3 Aquarius (6 degree orb).

Interpretation

The meaning of an aspect depends on the intrinsic nature of the planets in aspect and their sign placings. Who wants a trine of detrimented planets? Dignified planets in square might achieve more.

Aspect Lines

Lines to show aspects are sometimes drawn in the centre of the horoscope wheel, in different colours to show easy or difficult aspects. They can be helpful for beginners but are unnecessary - and even a hindrance - for an experienced astrologer. Aspects are recognisable at a glance due to the relationship of the planets by sign. For example, within acceptable orbs, planets in the same element trine each other, those in the same mode square each other; sextiles are two signs away, semi-sextiles are one sign away, a quincunx is an opposition, less a sign either side.

There's a simple rule for finding the semi-square and sesquiquadrate points of any planet: **add 15 degrees and go to the same degree in the next mode**. Remember that the modes run cardinal, fixed, mutable, cardinal etc. For example, in Freud's chart (p.94), Pluto is at 4 Taurus. Add 15 degrees = 19 Taurus. Taurus is a fixed mode, the next mode is mutable. The four semi-square and sesquiquadrate points are therefore at 19 degrees of the mutable signs, and Pluto at 4 Taurus is semi-square Neptune at 19 Pisces.

Aspect Grid

An aspect grid is a helpful way to record all the aspects in a horoscope.

	☽	☿	♀	♂	♃	♄	♅	♆	♆	☊	Asc.	MC
☉	⋎				∟		☌	✳				□
☽							□					✳
☿		⋎	△	✳	⋎	☌						□
♀					✳				☌			△
♂		☊		□				⊼				∟
♃			□									
♄							□		✳			
♅							✳					□
♆							∟					⊼
♆									☊			
☊												△

Asc.   MC

E.g.

The Sun is conjunct Uranus ☉ ☌ ♅

The Moon is square Neptune ☽ □ ♆

Mars is opposite Jupiter ♂ ☊ ♃

Sun is semisquare Jupiter ☉ ∠ ♃
(dissociate)

HERE IS A GRID, SHOWING FREUD'S ASPECTS.

77

ASPECT PATTERNS

Patterns of aspects between planets give a focus to interpretation. Well-known patterns are:

T-SQUARE

Frequently found. Two planets in opposition, each in square to a 3rd "handle" planet, which comes under maximum pressure.

Oliver Cromwell "Iron will and high moral purpose"
Any other planet trine or sextile with any part of the T-square "mediates" or releases the pressure.

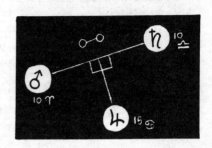

GRAND CROSS

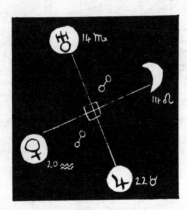

Two sets of oppositions, creating four squares, falling in one of the modes (cardinal, fixed or mutable). It symbolizes blockage and a life of struggle before success is attained. It is helped by any other planet mediating by easy aspect (trine, sextile).

Mao Tse-tung Fixed Cross (wide)

GRAND TRINE

Three planets, each in trine to the other, usually in the same element. Although trines are creative, this pattern has a reputation for over-emphasizing the element involved and for "getting in a spin".

Marlon Brando
a film legend

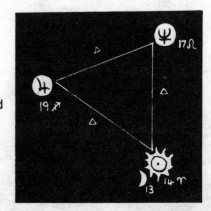

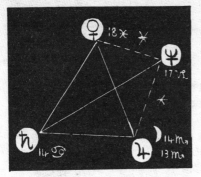

KITE

An extension of the Grand Trine with a 4th planet in opposition and two sextiles, acting as the **handle** of the kite. Potent, provided the opposition is mastered.

Jules Verne shows the imaginative power of a water Grand Trine in a Kite to Neptune (20,000 leagues under the sea!)

YOD (FINGER OF GOD, FINGER OF FATE)

Two planets in sextile, each quincunx a 3rd. The third planet is picked out and attracts peculiar situations and coincidences (*it's karmic!*)

Princess Diana
This *is where she connects with Charles!*

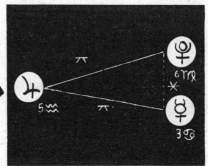

STELLIUM

Four planets or more in a daisy-chain of conjunctions. It emphasizes the sign and house in which it is placed. A key to understanding is the planet which rules the sign of the stellium.

Escher's work is like this Stellium

Bits and Bobs

Here are some other factors you will come across in the horoscope.

Planets Retrograde ℞

From an earth viewpoint planets (but not the Sun or Moon) can appear to go backwards (retrograde) in the zodiac for certain periods. The slower planets from Jupiter outwards are retrograde from between a third to a half of the year when the Sun is in the other half of the zodiac. The retrograde of Mercury, Venus or Mars is quite significant. It can modify or hinder their usual way of working, making their action less direct. Planets have a strong underlying influence on the day they reach a "station" and change direction (from direct motion to retrograde = **SR**; from retrograde to direct motion = **D** or **SD**).

The Moon's Nodes

- North Node (Dragon's Head) ☊
- South Node (Dragon's Tail) ☋

These have already been mentioned in talking about Stonehenge (pp.6-7). They form a major axis across the horoscope, especially if a planet is conjunct one of them. The North Node shows a direction to travel in, while the South Node is a place of danger or regression, something to leave behind.

Mutual Reception

This is where two planets are in each other's sign of rulership eg. Mars in Libra (ruled by Venus) and Venus in Scorpio (ruled by Mars). It indicates special talent related to those planets and shows them working together harmoniously. It counteracts an otherwise detrimented placing.

Element Balance

This can be revealing, especially when there is an element missing, implying an imbalance. Usually only the traditional planets are taken, and then the number of planets in each element (Fire, Earth. Air and Water) is totted up.

Bringing the Zodiac down to Earth

At any given moment the planetary positions and aspects in the zodiac are the same for everyone, all over the world. These positions reflect a broad **UNIVERSAL** symbolism.

For more specific interpretations, astrologers "cast" the **horoscope**, which is a diagram of the heavens as seen from a given place on the earth at a given instant.

The natal horoscope is cast for the moment of birth, but horoscopes can be cast for any event defined in time and place.

The Horoscope Framework

Horoscope construction fuses the language of astronomy into poetry and philosophy.

Imagine yourself as a baby at birth on the earth.

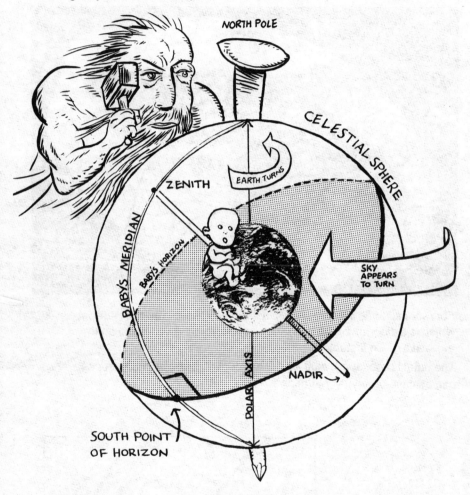

Human reality occurs within a **horizon** of meaning stretching around us. This divides the visible sky of consciousness from the invisible sky of unconsciousness beneath the earth.

The whole sky, the "universe", wheels round us from east to west once a day, drawing Sun, Moon, stars and zodiac across our horizon, symbolizing the round of changing human experience.

Directly above us is the **zenith**, at the top of our local sky. It symbolizes where we're headed and the future. Below, through the centre of the earth and out on the other side is the opposite point, the **nadir**. This is the past, our origin – and also a point of no return.

Running from the unmoving Polar Axis of the turning sky, through our zenith and nadir, and at right angles to our horizon, is the north-south circle of the **meridian**. This is our connection with the hub of the universe, and it is our line of time and history.

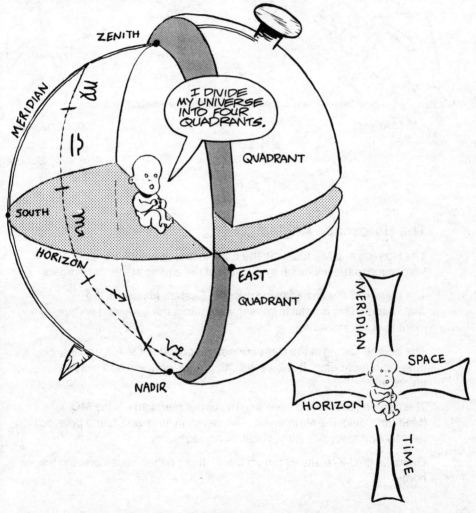

The meridian and horizon form a cross, carving out four quadrants in our local sky. This is the cross we bear, the fate we are allotted.

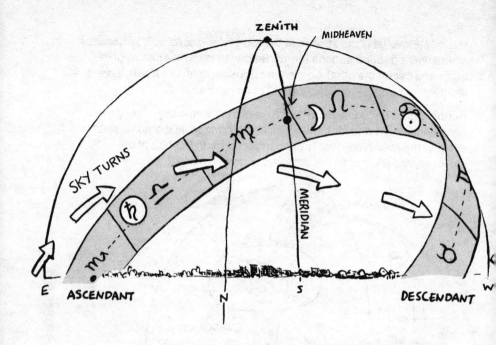

The Horoscope Angles

The Horizon and Meridian cut the Ecliptic at four points, pegging the horoscope to the universal symbolism of the zodiac at the four **Angles**.

The degree of the zodiac rising over the Eastern horizon is the **Ascendant**. This is what is coming-into-being, the body and unique identity of the individual.

The degree setting is the **Descendant**. Opposed to the Ascendant, it is passing-out-of-being. It shows the Other, thus partners and sexual union.

The degree culminating – passing the upper meridian – is the **MC** (Medium Coeli), the Midheaven. The meridian links zenith and pole, so the MC symbolizes destiny, vocation and authority.

Opposite the MC is the **IC** (Imum Coeli). It shows the ancestors and the home.

Each of the four quadrants is trisected to create the twelve **Houses** of the horoscope, showing particular departments of life.

The quadrants are usually unequal sizes in zodiac degrees, and although astrologers agree closely on the **interpretation** of the houses, there are many ways of performing the **maths** of quadrant trisection. This means competing "house systems" produce different zodiac positions for the intermediate (between angles) house cusps. Troublesome! The most prevalent system is that of **Placidus**, a 17th-century Italian monk, with its modern close derivative **Topocentric**.

Another approach abandons quadrant-trisection and simply counts off 12 equal 30-degree zodiac segments from the Ascendant to create the houses (**Equal-House system**).

The horoscope can be drawn in various ways.

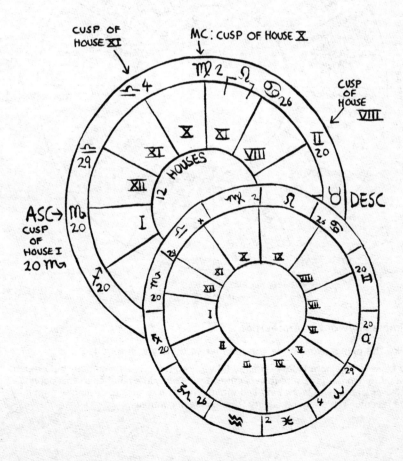

The Meaning of The Houses

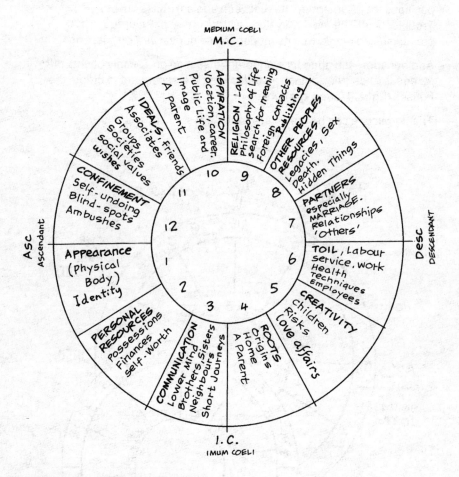

Simple keyword interpretation:

Take the **planet** working in the manner of the **sign**, in a **house**.

eg **Mars in Capricorn in 2nd** - energy (Mars) expressed in an ambitious but prudent way (Capricorn) in matters to do with finance (2nd). In a natal chart this could show an aptitude to work hard and attain long-term targets in dealing with money and resources. It's a good quality for a financial controller.

Keywords

Signs	Mode of working
Aries	pioneering, assertive
Taurus	building, possessing
Gemini	communication, dividing, questioning
Cancer	protecting, nurturing
Leo	creating, organizing, enjoying
Virgo	analysing, discriminating
Libra	balancing, harmonizing, reactive
Scorpio	penetrating, intense, secretive
Sagittarius	seeking, exploring, visionary
Capricorn	ambitious, controlling, prudent
Aquarius	principled, communal, detached
Pisces	self-sacrificing, devotional

Planets

Sun	Essence, self, creative principle, power, vitality, paternal function.
Moon	Response, fluctuation, instinct, habit, receptive, maternal function.
Mercury	Communication, intelligence, mind, self-expression.
Venus	Evaluation, love, relation, attraction.
Mars	Energy, will, desire, initiatory force, sex urge, self-assertion, anger.
Jupiter	Expansion, opportunity, preservation, protection.
Saturn	Limitation, form, containment.
Uranus	Revolution, disruption, dissociation.
Neptune	Nebulousness, idealism, fantasy, confusion, yearning.
Pluto	Destruction, elimination, regeneration, transformation.

Chart data used in this book:

Marlon Brando, 3 April 1924, 11:00 pm CST, Omaha, Nebraska, USA (41N17, 96W01).

Coronation of William I, Christmas Day, true local noon, Westminister, London, England (51N30, 0W07).

Oliver Cromwell, 25 April 1599 (OS), 5 May 1599 (NS), 3:00 am LMT (+/- 1 hour), Huntingdon, England (51N15, 0W12).

Princess Diana, 1 July 1961, 7:45 pm BST, Sandringham, England (52N50, 0E30). Another variant gives a time of 2:00 pm.

Bob Dylan, 24 May 1941, 9:05 pm CST, Duluth, Minnesota, USA (46N47, 92W07).

M. C. Escher, 17 June 1898, 7:18 am LMT, Leeuwarden, Netherlands (53N12, 5E46).

F. Scott Fitzgerald, 24 September 1896, 3:30 pm LMT, St Paul, Minnesota, USA (44N57, 93W06).

Henry Ford, 30 July 1863, 2:00 pm LMT (+/- 1 hour), Greenfield, Michigan, USA (43N11, 85W15).

Sigmund Freud, 6 May 1856, 6:30 pm LMT, Freiberg, Moravia (49N38, 18E09).

Henry VIII, 28 June 1491 OS, 8:45 am LMT, Greenwich, England (51N29, 0W00).

Carl Jung, 26 July 1875, 7:32 pm LMT, Kesswil, Switzerland (47N36, 9E19).

Lenin, 22 April 1870 (NS), time unknown, Simbirsk, Russia (54N17, 48E26).

Karl Marx, 5 May 1818, 2:00 am LMT, Trier, Germany (49N45, 6E06).

Benito Mussolini, 29 July 1883, 2:00 pm LMT, Dovia il Predappio, Italy (44N13, 12E02).

Margaret Thatcher, 13 October 1925, 9:07 am GMT, Grantham, England (52N56, 0W39); rectified from 9:00 am stated time.

Mao Tse-tung, 26 December 1893, 7:00 - 9:00 am LMT, Siangton, Hunau, China (27N55, 112E47).

Rudolph Valentino, 6 May 1895, 2:45 am MET, Castalleneta, Italy (40N53, 17E14).

Jules Verne, 8 February 1828, 12:00 pm LMT, Nantes, France (47N13, 1W33).

Duke of Wellington, 1 May 1769, 11:58 pm LMT, Dublin, Ireland (53N20, 6W15).

Horary Chart, "Should I Accept the Publishing Job?", 27 January 1995, 10:09 am, Isleworth, England (51N28, 0W20).

PART III INTERPRETING THE BIRTH CHART

Putting it all together

Combining planets, signs and houses is the ABC of horoscope interpretation. There are two broad approaches. The first, often given in modern textbooks, consists of **keywords and principles**; the second, characteristic of astrology in practice, involves **symbolic images and context**.

1. Keywords and Principles

The astrologer seeks ideal **cosmic principles** reflected in the world or in personality. Further, by finding **keywords** which approximate to the principle of each astrological factor, any combination in the horoscope can be given a theoretical interpretation.

Example: Uranus and Neptune in Sagittarius in the 10th, the principles of **revolution/disruption** and **idealism/fantasy** express in a **visionary/exploratory** (Sagittarius) way in career or vocation (10th). This package is then reworked into a natural-sounding interpretation.

THIS APPROACH IS LOGICAL AND EASY FOR THE BEGINNER, BUT IT CAN LACK VITALITY.

TENTH HOUSE

2. Symbolic Images and Context

In this approach, symbols are seen as haphazard poetic associations which reflect the particular subject matter. They have innumerable associations, concrete images and abstract concepts, but **no defining principles** apart from the astrological factors themselves.

The Uranus-Neptune example in Sagittarius is from the birthchart of Karl Marx, and one of its significations is undoubtedly Marx's near-mystical **goal of perpetual revolution**, his calling or ultimate ambition (10th).

Thumbnail Character Sketch

The **thumbnail character sketch** combines keywords for the **Sun, Moon and Ascendant** Signs into a "synthesis".

The Sun represents a person's essence, the guiding principle of their individual integrity. **The Ascendant** (appearance and identity) and **the Moon** (habit and response) can complement or mask this essence.

Example: *Margaret Thatcher*

Sun Libra, manifesting through Ascendant Scorpio, Moon Leo. The reactive rather than harmonious, nature of the Libran Sun is brought out by a tenacious and vengeful Scorpio Ascendant, and complemented by a regal and showy Moon in Leo. The Scorpio-Leo combination is powerful and domineering, even bullying, and this is how she appeared.

Compare Thatcher with: *Benito Mussolini*

Sun Leo, manifesting through Ascendant Scorpio, Moon Gemini. *Il Duce's* glorious – or boastful – Sun in royal Leo is complemented by a hypnotic Scorpio Ascendant and a Gemini Moon – brilliant for mass-communication and propaganda.

Try this on any horoscopes you can get your hands on. But how do we handle the whole chart?

The Order In Which To Interpret a Birth Chart

Don't try to interpret every planet, in every sign, in every house. It's boring – and ineffective. Instead, try to **locate significance** – find out what's important and unique about the chart. Use whatever you know about the person as the context to flesh out the symbolism.

Nine Easy Steps To Chart Interpretation

The first two steps provide a broad back-drop. The remainder paint a more specific picture. When looking at any planet, take account of its strength or weakness by sign.

Step 1. Get your thumbnail sketch.

Step 2. Check planets by element and mode. Is there any preponderance, or any missing element or mode?

Step 3. To find out what's special about **this** chart, go for specifics through the Ascendant ruler and see if anything strikes you about its sign, house or close aspect. This will highlight a fundamental theme of the life.

Step 4. Look at any planet on an angle (5 degree orb). This planet will dominate the life, most of all if it's on the Ascendant.

Step 5. See if any planet is on an intermediate house cusp (2 degree orb), emphasizing that house.

Step 6. Look for any close major aspect (1 degree orb), or any major conjunction, especially involving the Sun or Moon. This will be an important theme.

Step 7. Find aspect patterns. If these involve factors from Steps 3-6, the pattern is definitely significant and should be interpreted.

Step 8. Look for any planet which stands out because it's
  - a singleton (the only planet in one hemisphere)
  - has many strong aspects
  - is closely conjunct the Nodes or Part of Fortune.

Step 9. Consider whether a theme has emerged, repeated in different factors.

Let's try this now with Freud's birth chart.

Sigmund Freud Analysed

A MAJOR ASPECT PATTERN
IS A T-SQUARE (DISSOCIATE)
BETWEEN MARS, JUPITER
AND SATURN.

MARS AND VENUS
ARE IN MUTUAL
RECEPTION

MARS IS A SINGLETON
(ONLY PLANET IN EASTERN
HEMISPHERE) MARS, RULER
OF ASC. IS RETROGRADE
(MOVING BACKWARDS) IN
LIBRA IN THE 11th HOUSE

THE MOON IS AT
14°31' OF GEMINI
IN THE 8th HOUSE

MERCURY AND
URANUS IN WIDE
CONJUNCTION

ASCENDANT AT
7½° OF SCORPIO

THE SUN AND
URANUS ARE
CONJUNCT

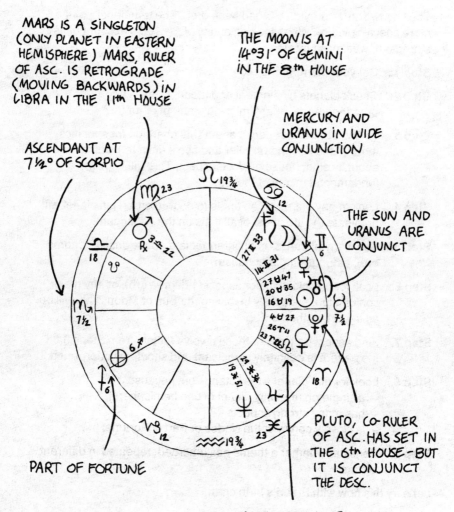

PART OF FORTUNE

PLUTO, CO-RULER
OF ASC. HAS SET IN
THE 6th HOUSE - BUT
IT IS CONJUNCT
THE DESC.

MOON'S NORTH NODE
(DRAGON'S HEAD)

Step-by-step through Freud's Chart

Steps 1 and 2: The background

Taurus Sun, Ascendant Scorpio, Moon Gemini

Scorpio rises – the sign of psychology, sexuality and death.

Freud's earthy, empirical Taurus Sun grounds these emotional realms through dogged persistence, building up a practice.

He is a medical man (Taurus-Scorpio), curious about mental processes (Moon Gemini).

There are no marked inequalities in elements or modes, so there's nothing to say about them.

Steps 3 and 4: Ascendant Rulers, Planets on Angles

Scorpio rising, ruled by Mars and Pluto

Pluto: The lord of the underworld, Pluto, dominates Freud's horizon and announces his life theme – the discovery of the unconscious.

It symbolizes his fascination with Thanatos (death instinct), and his desire to transform (Pluto) others (7th).

His marriage (7th) **doesn't** reflect this, but his significant partnerships (7th) with peers display the destructive power-struggle of Pluto detrimented in Taurus (look what happened to Freud's partners Breuer, Fliess, Jung).

Mars is **retrograde**, introverting energy, in the 11th house of collectives, colleagues, ideals and wishes. Freud's ideology of the sexual theory (Mars Libra 11th) founded a collectivity, the psychoanalytic community (11th house), but he had to fight (Mars), even with his friends (11th).

Step 5: There are no planets on intermediate cusps.

Step 6: Close aspects, major conjunctions

There are no very close aspects between planets, but look at the Sun-Uranus conjunction. This emphasizes the theme of the 7th – the Other – already shown by Pluto on the 7th cusp, and the Sun signifies Freud's vocation (it rules his MC). The conjunction with revolutionary Uranus shows genius but this is also his lifelong sense of being an outsider.

Step 7: Aspect Patterns

There is a T-square, dissociate, of Mars, Jupiter and Saturn, mediated by Mercury.

The struggle between Mars and Jupiter is the central axis and looks like Freud's "wish to perform a work of great magnitude".

JUPITER IN THE 5TH HOUSE SHOWS THE CHILD!

His creative work was inspired by his own children and by the imaginative realm of the child (the Oedipus Complex).

A key Freudian theme emerges in this T-square: the **unconscious wish** (Mars retrograde 11th) is **censored** (Saturn in Gemini in the unconscious 8th), but it manifests as wish fulfilment (Mars opposite Jupiter), especially through **free association** and **dream** (Jupiter in Pisces). The Mars-Saturn square also suggests an Oedipal theme, the desire (Mars) to kill (8th) the father (Saturn).

THE OUTLET OF THIS T-SQUARE TO MERCURY IS MY SOLUTION, THE GROUND OF PSYCHOANALYSIS — THE *TALKING CURE!*

Reading the symbolism this way, the T-square refers not only to Freud's own personality, but to the structure of his creative contribution.

Step 8: Other exceptional factors

Mars is a **singleton**, showing its importance as ruler of the Ascendant and as a driving force for Freud. It singles him out.

Step 9: Chart Themes

Interpretation is secured by "testimonies", a mirroring of themes in the horoscope. With Freud, the emphasis on the 7th and 8th houses is **visually** apparent, but the same thread is interwoven through the chart.

Ascendant ruler Mars in Libra is in the **7th sign** of relationship.

Pluto is on the **7th cusp** of partners.

Mars is in mutual reception with Venus, natural planet of relationship, and Venus rules the 7th house (Taurus is on the cusp).

Venus is herself highlighted by conjunction with the North Node.

Sexuality and the death instinct are shown by Scorpio, the 8th sign rising, with both the Moon and Saturn in the 8th house, and above all, an angular Pluto.

How much of our interpretation depends on the given context?

In practical astrology the answer is: quite a lot.

For example, both **Freud** and **Thatcher** have Ascendant Scorpio with its ruler Mars in Libra in the 11th House. This is like the Prime Minister as "first among equals" in her Cabinet, and similarly with Freud and his colleagues.

So Mars can be **sex** or **war**, and the 11th can be friends, politics or ideals, depending on the context.

On the other hand, without any context we could infer that both will fight for their ideals, even with colleagues (Mars, Libra, 11th).

MOVING THE BIRTHCHART ON

Timing Measures

The natal chart lasts a lifetime, but timing measures bring into play different features of its symbolism at different times of life. The main modern techniques are:

1. **Cycles and Returns**
2. **Transits**
3. **Progressions**

Let's start with **Cycles and Returns**.

Cycles: As planets move through the Zodiac, they complete their circuit of twelve signs in different periods of time. The cycles for Mercury and Venus vary, but each averages out to a year. Mars averages to about two years.

Jupiter	–	12 years
Saturn	–	29 years
Uranus	–	84 years
Neptune	–	165 years
Pluto	–	248 years

The cycles and part-cycles of the slower planets are especially important in marking out phases of life. How we interpret the cycles depends on the nature of the planet and how it is placed in the horoscope.

Returns: When a planet completes a cycle it **returns** to its natal position. With the exception of the Sun and Moon, it may have three or even five bites at the cherry if it retrogrades (turns back) after passing its birth position.

The **Solar Return** occurs each year, around your birthday, when the Sun completes a 360-degree cycle and returns to the degree it occupied at birth.

AND THAT'S WHY YOUR FRIENDS WISH YOU MANY *HAPPY RETURNS!*

A TRADITIONAL METHOD OF PREDICTION FOR THE COMING YEAR IS TO CAST A HOROSCOPE FOR THE EXACT INSTANT OF THE SOLAR RETURN.

THE SATURN CYCLE

The 29-year Saturn Return cycle shows a time of reckoning which puts individuals on their true path in life. It indicates responsibility, consolidation and the demand to "get real". Negatively, it may manifest as losing one's way, self-doubt, suffering and loss.

Religious myths often use 30 as the turning-point age when great teachers hear their calling.

Christ began his Mission at the age of 30 and **Prince Gautama Buddha** made his Great Renunciation in his thirtieth year.

And you?...

A SECOND SATURN RETURN OCCURS AT THE AGE OF 58. THIS SYMBOLISES THE ENTRY INTO THE LAST CHAPTER OF LIFE, FACING THE INEVITABILITY OF OLD AGE AND DEATH.

THE JUPITER CYCLE

Jupiter's twelve-year return symbolizes expansion and self-development, a search for something bigger and better, especially through travel, law, procreation, religion and philosophy. Jupiter may also symbolize excess and hubris but unhappy events on the Jupiter Return sometimes turn out to be blessings in disguise. People ruled by Jupiter – Sagittarius and Pisces – often follow a 12-year Jupiter rhythm. Do you?

One Jupiter Cycle in the Life of a Busy King

12 Feb 1533   **Jupiter Half Cycle**
(24 Sagittarius 24) first contact. Eighteen days earlier (25 January), Henry secretly married Anne Boleyn.

8 May 1527   **3rd Jupiter Return**
(24 Gemini 24) Nine days later (17 May), Henry started the legal process to dissolve his marriage to Catherine.

The religious struggles of **Henry VIII** (1491-1547) are bracketed by his **3rd and 4th Jupiter Returns**. His split with Rome was invoked by his desire to remarry in order to produce a male heir. Henry's birthchart shows why this cycle should show so strongly. Jupiter in Gemini (religious arguments) is strongly placed in his 10th house, opposite dissolving Neptune. Both of these planets rule his 7th house of marriage.

This Jupiter cycle times events in Henry's life very precisely. It also shows how the half-cycle may play into the theme.

24 ♃ ♐ 24

28 May 1533 Jupiter Half Cycle
(second contact, retrograde) Five days earlier (23 May), Henry's marriage to Catherine was annulled. This led to Clement VII's threat to excommunicate Henry – Jupiter opposite Jupiter!

19 April 1539 4th Jupiter Return
Within a month (May 1539) the Dissolution of the Great Monasteries completed Henry's struggle with the Church.

♃ 24 ♊ 24

THE URANUS CYCLE

Uranus has an 84 year cycle. Orbital eccentricity varies the half-cycle anywhere between 38 and 46 years.

The half-cycle gives the astrological mid-life crisis, symbolizing a now-or-never mood of reform or bust, awakening repressed desires. It may indicate liberation from past conditioning and a creative rebirth, or sudden traumas, splits and irresponsibility.

The psychologist **Carl Jung** (born 26 July 1875) underwent a psychotic collapse between 1913 and 1916, focused partly on the Uranus half-return in 1915.

The manufacturer **Henry Ford** (1863-1947) had Uranus in Gemini and in 1903, following his Uranus half-return, he founded the Ford Motor Company.

Ford died at the age of 84, within one day of his Uranus Return on 7 April 1947.

TRANSITS

As planets move in their cycles through the Zodiac, they pass over – or **transit** – planets and other significant points of the birth horoscope. Transits of the slower planets by conjunction and opposition are the most significant.

Transits are an easy, fast-food technique. You can find them by looking up the planets in the ephemeris for any particular date.

Transiting planets affect natal planets or factors according to their natures. For example ...

– Saturn opposing natal Mars **limits** (= Saturn) **desire** (= Mars).
– Jupiter conjunct natal Midheaven brings **expansion** (= Jupiter) in **career** (= MC).

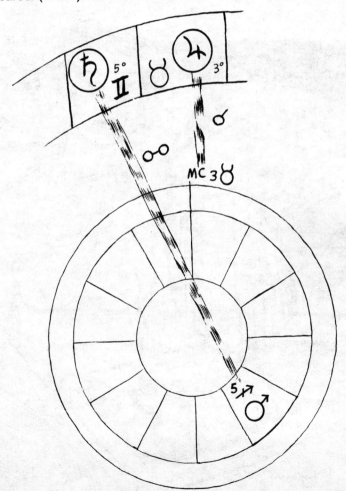

How transits act on natal factors

Jupiter transits   expand, liberate, begin things, allow prosperity.

Saturn transits   restrict, frustrate, consolidate, delay, end things, bring fear and responsibility.

Uranus transits   revolutionize, defy, separate, make redundant, strive for independence

Neptune transits   idealize, renounce, confuse, put at sea, sacrifice, deceive, distort, purify, transcend.

Pluto transits   transform, revive, destroy, purge, terrorize, deny, deepen.

Transits by the faster planets can be effective but are often limited in scope.

PROGRESSIONS – the serious stuff!

Secondary Progressions move the planets away from their birth positions, using a symbolic measure of time in which the two cycles of the Earth-Sun relationship, the DAY and the YEAR, reflect each other.

On average, the Sun progresses just under one degree every year of life, the Moon moves a degree a month and the other planets vary. Progressions are broadly operative for a year either side of exactitude, except for the Moon which is significant only for the month of its contact.

> PLANETS IN THE SKY *ONE* DAY AFTER BIRTH SIGNIFY LIFE CONDITIONS *ONE YEAR* AFTER BIRTH.

The Midheaven is progressed by the same number of degrees as the progressed Sun. The Ascendant is also moved on, but this is all getting too technical to go into here!

Significant changes occur when progressed planets make contact with natal planets.

For example, **Bob Dylan** (born 24 May 1941) has the Sun at 3 degrees Gemini and Mercury at 23 degrees Gemini. In 1961 he was twenty and his progressed Sun was therefore conjunct Mercury. That year, Dylan made it to Carnegie Hall, New York, and signed his first recording contract.

Margaret Thatcher declared war over the Falklands (April 1982) in the year that Mars – the war planet – progressed to her natal Ascendant.

Transits keyed in exacty: transit Mars crossed her natal Mars within hours of the Argentine invasion (a Mars Return), just as Saturn was crossing her natal Sun in Libra (a heavy decision).

THE MACHINE OF DESTINY

Timing measures give us insight into the chart's symbolism because we can see how it has worked out in the past. As the planetary cycles unfold in time, they appear to unfold human destiny and allow the possibility of prediction. Planetary motion is equated with fate. Remember Manilius (p. 22) and his immutable laws of fate?

Astrologers sometimes hit quite exact predictions using the timing measures, and because transits and progressions can be calculated with technical precision for any future date, it looks as if our fate is clockwork as well. Then we start to imagine the heavens as a terrible **Machine of Destiny**.

Referring to "trends" and "potentials" only fudges the issue. We will still imagine ourselves to be **fated** with a Saturn **trend**.

So can astrology predict?

Yes, but the astrologer never knows for sure **when** and in **what way** it will predict! This is because **planetary motions** and **planetary symbolism** are entirely different orders of phenomena.

As with all forms of divination, foreknowledge is possible only within a creative act which takes the context and purpose of the divination into account. Fortunately for everybody, astrology is an art of interpretation, not a deterministic science of causes.

In fact, the symbolic language of astrology makes the astrologer's universe a mysterious and poetic place . . .

Part IV: The Astrologer's Universe

The Great Ages

Astrology reads TIME and HISTORY through symbol.

The largest time-frame in practical astrology is the 25,868-year-cycle of PRECESSION of the Equinox, the 0 Aries point (see p30-31). This moves backwards through each of the twelve zodiacal fixed-star constellations, creating the "Great Ages" of around 2,000 years each.

The Age of Aries

The two brightest stars of the Aries constellation are Hamal (El Nath) and Sharaton. The Spring Point crossed the longitudes of these stars from 713BC to 446BC, and an "Arien" burst of new ideas and teachers transformed China (Confucius 6th century BC), Greece (rise of the Greek city states) and India (Gautama Buddha 7th century BC).

The Age of Pisces

We are now at the tail-end of Pisces and will enter the "Age of Aquarius" around 2300AD. The Equinox point reached the Knot Star (Al Rischa) that binds the Pisces fish in 111BC and in the Aries-Pisces overlap, Christ was born as the last Lamb (Ram) of the Age of Aries and the first Fish of sarificial Pisces

Jung claimed that the two fishes show Christianity's split between spirit and matter. The Equinox reached the first star of the second fish in 1817, and the rise of secular science in this era fulfills ancient predictions of "antichrist". Marx was also born in 1818

Signatures

Often when we look at the birthchart of someone famous, our context for interpretation is not their personal psychology or their ordinary life. What grabs our attention is the **things they stand for or have created**. These things will be found in the horoscope as symbolic pictures or **signatures**. We've already made this type of interpretation for Freud's sexual theory, shown in the T-square in his birthchart. Here's another striking example.

Karl Marx was born a few hours before a Solar Eclipse in Taurus, the 2nd sign, and the eclipse factors are in a conjunction in his 2nd house (Dragon's Head, Moon, Sun). At the personal level, this could be problems with earnings (2nd, Taurus), or a need to find new values (New Moon in 2nd) in his life. But who cares? Look at the symbolism of TAURUS, the Bull = CAPITAL.

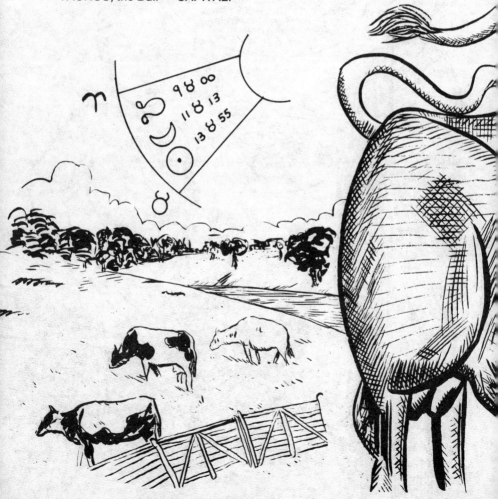

Capital and **cattle** are from the same Latin root **caput** – head (= head of cattle). Latin **pecus** for cattle also gives us **pecuniary**. **Fee** is from Gothic **faihi**, cattle. Now we see the association of Taurus the Bull with cash, economics and "value".

So the **eclipse in Taurus** is the **eclipsing of Capitalism** and Marx's great work, **DAS KAPITAL**.

Signatures show the Poetry of Astrology.

POPULAR ASTROLOGY

The First Columns

Since the 17th century, there has been a tradition of popular almanacs such as Old Moore's. This century has seen in addition the rise of the star-sign – strictly Sun-sign – in newspaper columns.

When Princess Margaret, sister of Queen Elizabeth, was born (21 August 1930), the *Sunday Express* published her horoscope, drawn up by R.H. Naylor (1889-1952). Its popularity led to the first astrology column on **5 October 1930**. Naylor also predicted danger to British aircraft, and that day the R-101 airship crashed in France on her maiden flight, shocking the nation.

Today, newspaper and magazine astrology is more concerned with guidance and personality types than with predicting disaster. It is based on broad astrological **signatures** for each of the twelve zodiac types. How?

Solar Houses

The usual method is **solar houses**. To generate readings for each sign for a specific time period, it is placed on the eastern, rising point. Houses are created from this point by successive signs.

For example: a Full Moon at 10 degrees Gemini, conjunct Jupiter.

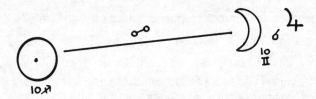

This line-up symbolizes opportunities, perhaps through conflict. It falls in the 1st and 7th houses (self and others) for a Sagittarian individual, but in the 4th and 10th houses (home and career) for Pisceans.

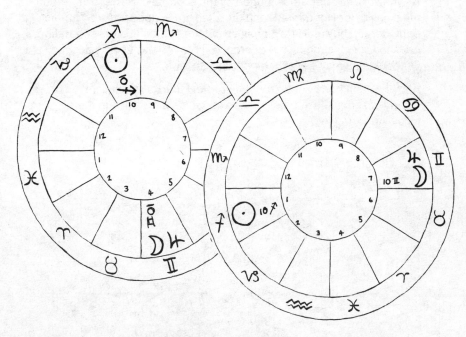

Producing a relevant text with guiding precepts for one-twelfth of the population is a difficult symbolic task. Sun-sign columns are criticized by sceptics and some "serious" astrologers, but like music astrology has both a pop and a more serious form.

HORARY ASTROLOGY

Astrology's ability to paint a symbolic picture finds full expression in a **horary chart**. This is a horoscope cast for the time and place when an astrologer is asked a specific question. Horary's distinct method and terminology aims to answer the question or determine the outcome of the issue.

Planets become symbolic representatives or **significators**.

The Querent (the person asking) is signified by the planet ruling the sign on the Ascendant.

The Quesited (the issue asked about) is signified by the planet ruling the relevant house cusp (eg money 2nd).

The Moon is a "universal co-significator". It usually co-signifies the querent, as well as the situation as a whole.

A "yes" or "no" answer is judged by the doctrine of **perfection**. When the significators for querent and quesited are in good applying aspect, unhindered, they indicate a positive outcome. Significators separating, or in no aspect, suggest the querent will not achieve what is desired. Other planets may assist or hinder by aspect.

Above all, the horary chart must be **radical**, i.e. its symbolism must clearly describe the situation asked about, as we will see in the following example.

Should I Accept the Publishing Job?

An unemployed woman was waiting for the result of an interview for a personnel job.

Here's how the situation looks in a horary chart. The chart is **radical** – it describes her situation, with Mars, Ascendant ruler, in the 6th house of work but retrograde – not working! The Moon as co-significator for her is in Sagittarius on the 9th house cusp of publishing.

Will she get the personnel job? There is no perfection (i.e. no applying aspect) of Mars or Moon (querent) with planets ruling the 6th (work) or 10th (vocation). Mercury is also retrograding from a recent opposition of Mars (querent). Mercury indicates the personnel job (ruling intercepted Virgo 6th), and describes the interview and lack of news. A separating opposition does not suggest future success.

She accepted the offer to begin work one week later. She subsequently heard from her employment agency that the personnel company wanted to see more CVs, so they had gone cold on her. She wrote to the astrologer soon after.

The two helpful girls are proof positive of the Moon-Venus conjunction – two female planets in eager Sagittarius on the 9th of foreigners and publishing!

A field of omens and divination...

Horary technique looks like the Machine of Destiny on tap, but fortunately, good radical horaries are occasional and come by grace, not will. Horary astrology is more like divination than science, and Ptolemy's idea of a seed-moment at birth cannot be satisfactorily applied to the "birth" of a question.

Horary has been attacked by **astrologers** – Ptolemy, Placidus, Morin de Villefranche. Al Biruni sums up the objection...

HERE ASTROLOGY THREATENS TO TRANSGRESS ITS PROPER LIMITS... WHERE THE ASTROLOGER IS ON ONE SIDE AND THE SORCERER ON THE OTHER, YOU ENTER A FIELD OF OMENS AND DIVINATION WHICH HAS NOTHING TO DO WITH ASTROLOGY.

Since the 1970s, horary has undergone a revival. In addition, **psychological horary** is a modern innovation which uses the horary method to bring to light unconscious motivations and desires.

125

MEDICAL ASTROLOGY

Astrology is used to diagnose disease through the Zodiac-planets-body link. Treatment was traditionally given through herbal remedies, derived from the theory of correspondences and the doctrine of sympathy or antipathy. For example, by sympathy, a Venus herb such as lady's mantle is used for gynaecological conditions. By antipathy, a warm Sun herb such as St John's Wort counters a cold, Saturnine depression.

The **Decumbiture** chart is a horoscope cast for the onset of illness. It symbolizes the patient and his or her disease, its future development, its times of crisis and its possible cure.

The English herbalist **Nicholas Culpeper** (1616-1654) is the master of the decumbiture approach. He cast the horoscope for the moment of receiving a patient's urine and used this and the urine for diagnosis and treatment.

Culpeper battled with the professional élitism of the medical profession which had a growing disdain for both astrology and traditional country remedies. Yet Culpeper's Herbal of plants and planetary correspondences has been in print almost continually since it was published in 1653!

The Decumbiture Method has been revived in modern astrology for **diagnosis**. Prescribing **treatment** requires further skills such as herbalism. The medical profession is as hostile to astrological herbalists today as it was to Culpeper. As a consequence, their practice is frequently underground and furtive.

RELOCATION

In a global society, astrological techniques have evolved accordingly. A **Relocation Horoscope** is cast for the birth time, but for any place of importance. It is especially useful for individuals living in foreign countries and for financial astrology and international markets. The relocated horoscope will show what issues arise for an individual or organisation in that particular place. Locations with planets on the horizon or meridian at the birth moment are suggestive of prosperity or danger, according to the nature of the planet.

Example: **WELLINGTON** had fortunate Jupiter in his natal 10th house. He was born in Dublin but when he achieved his famous victory over Napoleon at Waterloo, by relocation, Jupiter becomes conjunct the Part of Fortune on the Mid-Heaven, **exactly** trine and sextile the new horizon.

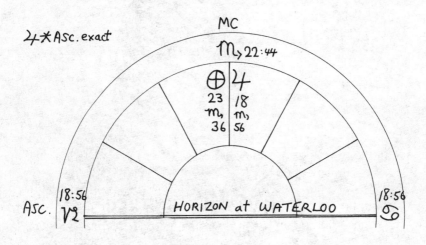

Astro*Carto*Graphy is a way of charting the rising and culminating of planets at the birth moment throughout the world. These are shown as lines running across a world map. Crossing points of two or more planets are especially potent.

BIRTH CONTROL

Astrological Birth Control is another modern technique. Its chief exponent was a Czechoslovakian doctor, Eugen Jonas (born 6 November 1928).

Jonas asserts that a woman has **two** fertility cycles each month: the monthly ovulation cycle, plus a **Moon-Phase cycle**, based on the Sun-Moon relationship at birth. Conception can occur on **either** cycle, even during menstruation!

In 1968, Jonas researched at the government-funded Astra Research Centre in Nitra, Czechoslovakia.

IT CLAIMED THAT 1,252 WOMEN USED ITS METHODS FOR A YEAR WITH 97.7% SUCCESS.

The Moon-Phase method was also used for sex selection, and both infertility and problem pregnancies were helped by ensuring conception took place only on the Moon-Phase cycle.

In 1970, Astra Nitra was closed down by the Soviet authorities. Attempts at replication have not succeeded, but astrologers find the method sometimes works in individual cases.

How to cope with Twins...

Twins have always been troublesome for astrologers. Non-identical twins who lead different lives are frequently born within minutes of each other, with virtually identical horoscopes. Even more problematic, modern fertility treatments and a Caesarian can produce sextuplets in under ten minutes.

Many astrologers assert that even a degree on the Ascendant can make all the difference, especially if we use ultra-fine techniques like minor aspects, harmonics and mid-points. But (as Augustine spotted over 1500 years ago) if such small changes make a huge difference for twins, it throws doubt on our ability to interpret the horoscope of someone who is **not** a twin, given that we can rarely be sure of the exact time of birth.

For a non-twin's horoscope, astrologers expect some modification from moving the Ascendant a couple of degrees within the same sign, but not a total change in basic character.

This is a problem for the classical tradition which got stuck with a literal-minded notion of astrological influences. A modern approach which works in practice accepts that the astrologer is reading the horoscope symbols **in context** and drops the theoretical notion of two separate horoscopes.

Time twins

Time twins, when people are born at the same time from different mothers, often produce fascinating symbolism. Sigmund Freud was born on a different continent but within minutes of Robert Peary (Cresson PA. 17:17 UT 6 May 1856). Freud discovered the Unconscious and Peary discovered the North Pole. Which is metaphor for which?

COMPATIBILITY

Studying the compatibility of individuals by comparing their birthcharts is known as **synastry** ("with the stars").

At its broadest level, individuals with the **same element** are compatible. Contrasting elements have varied psychological "chemistry" . . . fire makes water boil, water nourishes earth, earth suffocates fire, air lets fire breathe, makes water bubble . . . and so on.

The Venus sign also describes who attracts us – Venus in Aquarius likes Aquarians, and so on.

Inter-Aspects

Planetary aspects between charts are crucial. A woman's Saturn opposite a man's Mars rebuffs (Saturn) his desire (Mars). A mother's Jupiter conjunct a child's Mercury expands (Jupiter) communication skills (Mercury).

Remember the Das Kapital eclipse in **MARX's** birth chart? It's **LENIN** who is the **interpreter** of it.

Marx Moon   **11** Taurus
Marx Sun   **13** Taurus

Lenin's **Mercury**, **12** Taurus

Synastry can apply to any type of relationship and it has been used – controversially – to decide job applicants. Links between people and company charts are also taken into account.

The Cosmic Marriage

The most powerful inter-aspect is a Sun-Moon conjunction, known as a **cosmic marriage**. The two individuals are two halves of a whole.

FREUD and **JUNG** had this.

Freud's Sun at 16 Taurus, conjunct Jung's Moon at 15 Taurus. Freud (Sun) hoped to shine through Jung (Moon), but Jung could not simply reflect Freud's light. The father and mother (Sun and Moon) of analysis went their separate ways, but their work is two halves of a whole.

MUNDANE ASTROLOGY

Mundane astrology studies world events and politics. It uses horoscopes for nations, events and political leaders.

For example, an important horoscope for England is that of the crowning of William the Conqueror at Noon, 25 December 1066, Westminster Abbey. It still gives a thumbnail sketch of the English!

Sun in Capricorn in the 10th – reserved, conservative, traditional, class-conscious – bowler hats and grey suits.

Moon in Pisces in the 12th – passive islanders, emotionally withdrawn, fish and chips.

England has always been known as a belligerent Aries country from its assertive **Aries Ascendant**, through which Sun and Moon express. The Capricorn Sun fights for empires. The Pisces Moon drinks, becomes a lager lout and fights for nothing. Both World Wars and the Falklands were described by Mars progressions.

Diana Eclipsed

Prominent individuals often have synastry with their nation's chart. For example, Princess Diana, shy Di, has her Sun at 9 Cancer, conjunct the 1066 IC, **opposite** and in conflict with the nation's dutiful 10th house Capricorn Sun. On 30 June 1992, one day before Diana's birthday, **an eclipse of the Sun** at 8 Cancer fell on this Diana – 1066 contact. That month, Andrew Morton's revelations in his book on Di shook the Royal Family and the British psyche to the roots.

On 9 December, her separation from Charles was formally announced to Parliament. That night, a total eclipse of the Moon was visible at midnight on the London meridian. The Roman goddess Diana – the Moon – was eclipsed. She could never now be Queen. This eclipse fell at 18 Gemini, on the marriage point (Descendant) of her own horoscope!

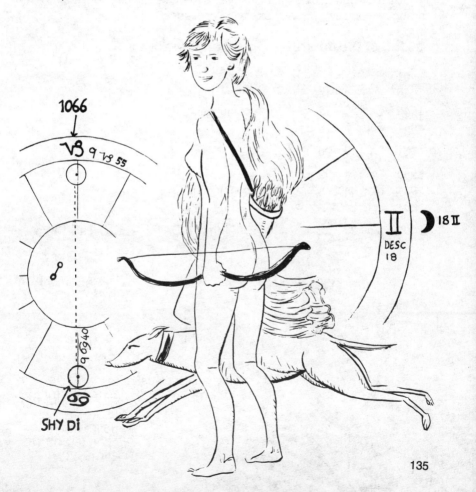

Mundane Cycles

Mundane Astrology also uses the planetary cycles of Jupiter, Saturn and the Outer Planets.

The Zeitgeist and the Jupiter-Saturn Cycle

The twenty-year Jupiter-Saturn conjunction is part of an 800-year cycle through the elements (see the Star of Bethlehem, page 35). Every twenty years, their conjunction marks the **zeitgeist**, "the spirit of the age". Individuals who epitomize this often have synastry with the conjunction and its moment. In the Roaring Twenties, the conjunction fell on Rudolph Valentino's horizon, whilst F. Scott Fitzgerald's Sun was conjunct the Mercury of the moment. In the Yuppy Eighties, it fell on Thatcher's Mars.

The Jupiter-Saturn opposition, ten years after the conjunction, marks a swing of mood away from the previous decade.

Dates of the Jupiter-Saturn Conjunctions:

1921	Sep 10	26 ♍	
1940	Aug 8	14 ♉	
1940	Oct 20	12 ♉	triple conjunction
1941	Feb 15	9 ♉	
1961	Feb 19	25 ♑	
1980	Dec 31	9 ♎	
1981	Mar 4	8 ♎	triple conjunction
1981	Jul 24	4 ♎	
2000	May 28	22 ♉	

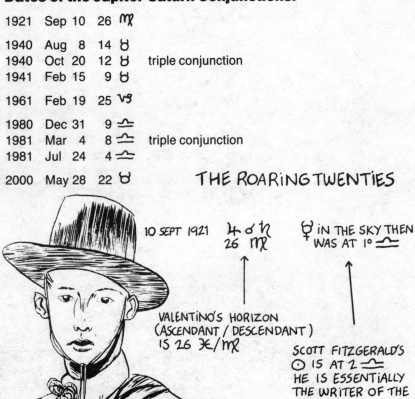

THE ROARING TWENTIES

10 SEPT 1921   ♃ ☌ ♄
26 ♍

☿ IN THE SKY THEN
WAS AT 1° ♎

VALENTINO'S HORIZON
(ASCENDANT / DESCENDANT)
IS 26 ♓/♍

SCOTT FITZGERALD'S
☉ IS AT 2 ♎
HE IS ESSENTIALLY
THE WRITER OF THE
TWENTIES

Saturn-Neptune and Socialism

The discovery of Neptune took place during the year of a Saturn-Neptune conjunction (1846). Neptune is associated with Socialism and Communism and the Saturn-Neptune cycle marks significant stages of their development. Note the pattern of Saturn-Neptune conjunctions in the 20th century:

one conjunction only
1917   1 Aug   –   Russian Revolution (Feb 1917)

triple conjunction
1952   21 Nov
1953   1 May   –   Death of Stalin (March 1953)
1953   22 July

triple conjunction
1989   3 Mar
1989   24 June
1989   13 Nov   –   Collapse of Soviet Bloc: the Berlin Wall came
                          down on 9 November!

Note: This is also the **exact** half-way point of the Jupiter-Saturn cycle, marking the Zeitgeist of the new decade of the nineties. Jupiter was opposite Saturn on **14 November**.

P.S. The next Saturn-Neptune conjunction won't be until 2026!

FINANCIAL ASTROLOGY

Financial astrologers believe that the Jupiter-Saturn cycle of economic growth (Jupiter) and recession (Saturn) is triggered by faster-moving planets like Venus. This gives a more specific focus to the Kondratieff 47-60 year economic cycle.

Planetary **stations** also reverse stock market trends, e.g. Mars retrograde in bad aspect to an outer planet heralds a fall. All such factors are related to the horoscopes of companies and individuals, alongside transits and progressions.

And now . . . remember Das Kapital and the Bulls? (page 116). Here's something for money-loving Taureans everywhere. Many of the world's most important financial institutions have a Taurus emphasis.

Bank of England	–	Sun	15 Taurus
World Bank	–	Moon	15 Taurus
Swiss Franc	–	Sun	16 Taurus

Stock Exchanges:

–	London	(14 July 1773)	–	Moon	22	Taurus
–	New York	(17 May 1792)	–	Sun	27	Taurus
–	Amsterdam	(17 May 1876)	–	Sun	26	Taurus
–	London	(18 May 1901)	–	Sun	26	Taurus
–	Tokyo	(15 May 1878)	–	Sun	24	Taurus

. . . AND HORSE-RACING

Astrology can be used for any form of speculation, including horse-racing. A chart is cast for the official start of the race to see if it has a prominent theme. A "winning" horse is chosen with a name to fit the theme. Sometimes, the jockey's colours and the handicap weight is linked to the chart's symbolism.

Example

Last Suspect, 50-1 Grand National winner 1985. This was chosen by many astrologers through the symbolism of Saturn, planet of time and endings, in suspicious and secretive Scorpio, exactly conjunct the IC.

This sort of astrology gets mischievous if it's pushed too hard. It can produce spectacular wins – and total failures!

RACING POST: Friday 9 December 1988

. . . we recently investigated The Gambling and Spirituality Workshop . . . They specialize in big races, apparently, and in the last couple of years have come up with Don't Forget Me (Guineas at 9-1 plus Bellotto for the forecast), Unite (Oaks at 11-1), Reference Point (Derby and Leger) and Rhyme 'N' Reason (National).

This year, their Classic strike rate has been slightly less spectacular, although they did all make a killing by backing Bellafella each way for the Guineas at 100-1. Don't laugh unless your system works any better.

THE MODERN ASTROLOGER

So astrologers poke their noses into everything and generally agree
about their symbolic language. However, their sense of purpose differs
widely. Most who give readings to others are a mixture of the following
main types.

Different Astrologies

Mrs Moon does a bit of everything – astrology, cards, crystals
clairvoyance etc., and isn't interested in theoretical concepts.

The Spiritual Astrologer often vaguely Theosophical, into karma and
reincarnation.

The Computer Astrologer. This is a descendant of Alan Leo's shilling horoscopes. Pages and pages of description, all about **you**! A pop, mail-order astrology which collates pre-written interpretations of chart factors by computer. Sometimes helpful but suffers from lack of context.

The Traditional Astrologer often has a stoic, fated approach and believes astrology is predictive and world-oriented. This astrologer privileges the horoscope and uses horary and traditional craft methods. He or she is not interested in psychology but may analyse character traits.

The Psychological Astrologer:

Modern astrology has gained in strength and popularity by linking with psychology. Psychological astrologers use the horoscope as a psycho-therapeutic or analytic tool, seeing it as a **map of the psyche**. Depending on the particular approach (Jung, Assagioli etc.), the horoscope shows complexes, archetypes, scripts, sub-personalities etc.

The Humanistic Astrologer originated in the USA. He or she sees the chart as a "seed-packet", indicating the individual's highest potential, and aims to nurture the client's soul-growth. Optimistic and ever-hopeful but often vague.

The Counselling Astrologer may or may not be a trained counsellor. He or she establishes an on-going relationship, using the chart to open up key issues for discussion. This astrologer is not predictive or prescriptive, privileging the client and the counselling process.

The Consultant Astrologer will pick and mix the above positions, using traditional and modern techniques, and is sympathetic to psycho-analysis and philosophy.   There are two identifiable styles . . .

● **Science-friendly**, with a rational, objective approach. Often uses modern techniques such as mid-points and harmonics [*see Little Dictionary].

● **Divinatory**, sees astrology as a form of divination, similar to the I Ching or Tarot, and probably uses horary.
Fundamentally, an up-market Mrs Moon.

If you visit an astrologer

* see Appendix page 171 for further information

Most professional astrologers have a fixed-length session and a set fee.
Some do written work, some give phone consultations. Face-to-face is
usual, with or without taping. Expect natal astrology unless otherwise
specified.

Choose the right type of astrologer

During the consultation

Some natal astrologers start with their analysis of character and possible events, then get you to respond. Others want you in the conversation from square one. Either way, expect a two-tier process. First the astrologer **negotiates the symbol** by testing out possible interpretations.

THIS STAGE IS OFTEN ATTACKED BY CRITICS AS THE *"BARNUM EFFECT"* - GENERAL TRUTHS THAT EVERYONE ASSENTS TO.

BUT THAT CRITICISM ONLY COVERS PART OF WHAT HAPPENS.

As the interpretation begins to bite, the astrologer will **speak from the symbol** as this becomes fleshed out in the exact context of your life circumstances. That's when you can expect unambiguous statements, precision and some predictive power.

So what can astrology do for us?

1. Self-knowledge. It makes us aware of our psychic make-up and helps us to see patterns in our lives. An hour with Mrs Moon can raise core issues that would take months to arrive at in therapy. Solving them is not so easy!

2. Confirmation. It confirms our sense of ourselves and the timeliness of our actions – when to sow, when to reap.

3. Creates meaning. Symbols bring meaning and give a sense of the sacred. Jung says they activate the unconscious and heal the psyche.

4. Poetry and Fun. Symbols open up poetry and imagination. They're also fun.

5. Problem solving. Astrology evokes lateral thinking and reveals connections we couldn't otherwise make.

6. It predicts the line of good fortune. It helps us to find the line of good fortune in practical matters and complex human relations.

PART V THE MODERN DEBATE

What is the Future for Astrology?

Wherever astrologers poke their heads above the parapets, there are enemies waiting to cut them down. The attack from Christianity is most often fronted by Fundamentalists, who frighten tolerant institutions like Planetariums and Education Authorities into dropping any presentation of astrology. But for a display of blind hostility, with few honourable exceptions, the performance of institutional science carries the day.

The biggest modern attack on astrology occurred in 1975, when the **Humanist** magazine of America published "Objections to Astrology", signed by "186 leading scientists", including eighteen Nobel Prizewinners.

So does astrology have any scientific evidence at all?

There are many established "cosmobiological" connections between the Solar System and life on earth which may have percolated through into astrological symbolism. This is obvious with lunar lore, as with the phenomenon of the monthly menstrual cycle, (menses = Moon). But this is a long way away from horoscopes.

There have been **big flops** in astrology experiments. Key studies have come up with zero results, notably the 1970s' study of horoscopes of 311 New York Suicides. However, the most impressive scientific work has been done by **Michel Gauquelin** (1928-1991), **and his wife Françoise**. Gauquelin trained in psychology and statistics.

FROM 1950, I METHODICALLY GATHERED FRENCH BIRTH DATA (WHICH GIVES THE TIME ON THE BIRTH CERTIFICATE) FOR THOUSANDS OF PROFESSIONALS IN CAREFULLY DEFINED GROUPS.

Gauquelin found that for eminent professionals there is a pattern of planets in "hot zones". These zones are the area of sky just after rising (above the Asc.) and culminating (the MC), and to a lesser extent at the opposite points (near the Desc. and IC). Further, the planets are **different** for different professions!

Here is one of his famous findings, the **Mars effect** at the birth of 570 French sports champions:

Gauquelin's sectors are like an 18-house horoscope (instead of the conventional twelve houses).

If Mars at birth gave no indication of a baby becoming a sports champion, then we would expect around 32 sports champions each sector (like the dotted line). It's more than 1000-1 against deviations as strong as this coming up "by chance".

Gauquelin established similar patterns for the following eminent European professionals.

Moon – writers and politicians
Venus – writers
Mars – athletes, soldiers
Jupiter – actors, soldiers, writers
Saturn – doctors, scientists

Is culture split between the musical/artistic and the scientific imaginations? If we take tough-minded Mars and Saturn for these groups we can actually demonstrate the reality of this "two cultures" divide.

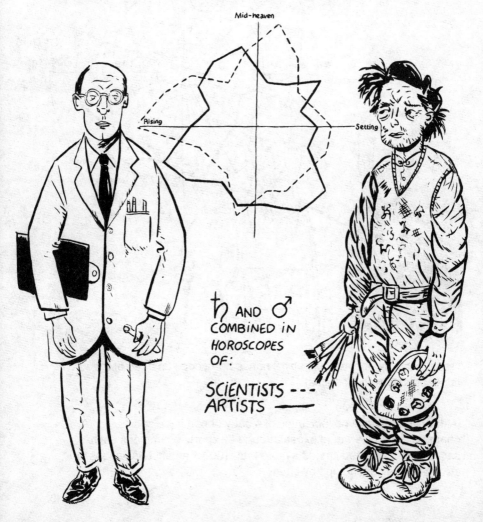

♄ AND ♂ COMBINED IN HOROSCOPES OF:

SCIENTISTS - - -
ARTISTS ―――

Gauquelin has established statistical significance in some categories at better than 1,000,000-1 against chance, impressive even for laboratory science.

Gauquelin's methods have never been materially faulted, or "disproved". All the raw data has been published and the methods used fully described, in English and French.

But what is marvellous about these findings is their compatibility with traditional planetary interpretations. Mars goes with soldiers, but so does Jupiter for the "top brass". Mars is the will to win of the solo athlete. Jupiter has always ruled actors, and melancholic Saturn's fit for the unemotional and cautious scientist is equally perfect. It seems likely that the professions follow indirectly from **temperament types** indicated by the planets at birth.

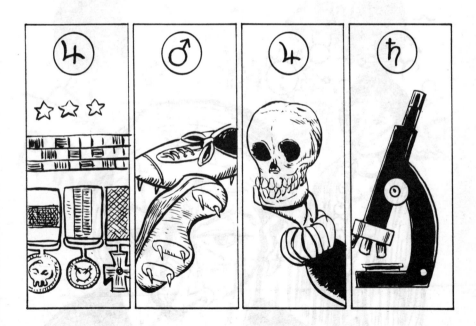

Testing horoscope interpretation:

Between 1959 and 1961 the US psychologist Vernon Clark tested astrologers' abilities to pick up biographical details from the birth horoscope.

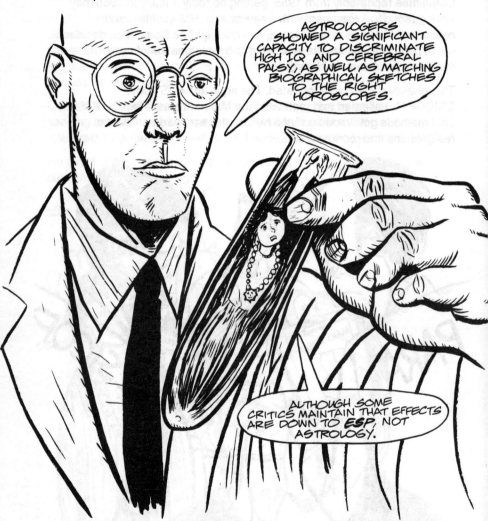

ASTROLOGERS SHOWED A SIGNIFICANT CAPACITY TO DISCRIMINATE HIGH IQ AND CEREBRAL PALSY, AS WELL AS MATCHING BIOGRAPHICAL SKETCHES TO THE RIGHT HOROSCOPES.

ALTHOUGH SOME CRITICS MAINTAIN THAT EFFECTS ARE DOWN TO *ESP*, NOT ASTROLOGY.

Repeat experiments proved unsatisfactory from a science-research perspective. Some have failed, others have shown a plus for astrology. But it's not clear why astrologers succeed sometimes and fail sometimes. Since the positive results outweigh the negative, there is **something** worth studying here.

Shawn Carlson's Experiment

The most publicized – and damaging – Vernon Clark-type test was conducted by Shawn Carlson at Berkeley, California (1981-2). Astrologers' judgments were tested against Personality Inventories (derived from a psychological questionnaire) for the test subjects.

The astrologers failed.

However, Carlson's methodology disintegrated, for example when a control group of non-astrologers produced crazy non-random results. Yet despite glaring weaknesses, the experiment was published without query in **Nature** (Dec 1985), together with the unscientific conclusion that this "clearly refutes the astrological hypothesis".

Institutional science gives astrology a NO-WIN situation. It's the Nelson syndrome – astrology simply won't be looked at.

Research into astrology is

a) **avoided wherever possible**, but failing that, it is
b) quoted **only** if it does not prove astrology, and
c) **rubbished** or **ignored** if it proves a hint of astrology.

Any test, however rigorous, that proves astrology is faulty by definition, but a sloppy test with negative results is fine for **Nature**. The claim that astrology has "no proof" is then reasserted and fed to the media. Scientists found straying may be quietly leaned on . . .

Symbolic thinking doesn't match the rational-scientific consensus about reality. The problem isn't about evidence – it's a battle of belief-systems.

Even done properly, modern science couldn't substantiate more than a fragment of astrology, much of which is essentially unprovable. Like art or language, symbolism reaches beyond the objective and empirical realm.

Many astrologers turn away from science and towards Depth Psychology, especially that of Carl Jung (1875-1961). His conception draws astrology back to its connection with Plato's IDEAS.

Jung's theory of Archetypes – structures underlying consciousness – explains the power of astrological symbolism to work in the imagination. The signs of the zodiac are therefore twelve "archetypal images" or manifestations of the collective unconscious.

Jung and Astrology

So how does astrology work, according to Jung? In 1930 he coined the term **synchronicity** – an "acausal connecting principle" – to describe meaningful coincidence. This involves qualitative time.

WHATEVER IS BORN OR DONE IN THIS MOMENT OF TIME HAS THE QUALITY OF THIS MOMENT OF TIME.

Although he later ditched this formulation, it remains a favourite with astrology authors. It fits with Ptolemy's ether, conveying heavenly changes instantaneously in the seed-moment. But Jung derived synchronicity from his understanding of astrology in the first place, so we're going round in circles!

ASC

In the early 1950's Jung tried to show synchronicity through his **marriage experiment** on horoscopes of couples, seeking three traditional compatibility contacts: Moon-Sun, Moon-Horizon and Moon-Moon. Something odd happened …

The first batch of data showed a statistically significant contact of Moon conjunct Ascendant. The second batch produced Moon conjunct Sun. The last batch gave Moon conjunct Moon. Together the results cancelled out – yet Jung saw that **separately** they mirrored the three combinations he was seeking. This led him to synchronicity version two, implicating the observer in the things observed.

A *SECRET MUTUAL CONNIVANCE* EXISTS BETWEEN THE MATERIAL AND THE PSYCHIC STATE OF THE ASTROLOGER.

Synchronicities occur when archetypal contents are "constellated" – i.e. erupt into consciousness. The Great Ages, defined in relation to constellations in the sky, illustrate this process on a vast collective scale (see pp114–115).

The Symbolic Attitude

Jung locates astrology not in a wholly physical world but in a psycho-physical reality of human **meaning**. This is why methods from the physical sciences are inappropriate in understanding astrology.

Symbols are the medium for the constellation of archetypes, and a **special type of thinking** is involved in seeing them. Jung refers to this as the "symbolic attitude".

Dane Rudhyar (1895-1985), the major figure of "humanistic astrology", was influenced by Jung's approach.

WHETHER A THING IS A SYMBOL OR NOT DEPENDS CHIEFLY UPON THE ATTITUDE OF THE CONSCIOUSNESS CONSIDERING IT.

IT IS FOR THE INDIVIDUAL TO LET SYMBOLS ORGANISE THEMSELVES INTO SIGNIFICANCE.

The "special thinking" required for the symbolic attitude is seen by Jung and others as related to **mythopeic thought**, the myth-making consciousness characteristic of primitive societies. The key to this type of thought is what to us seems to be its "subjective" and emotional component. The anthropologist Lucien Lévy-Bruhl (1857- 1939) referred to the **participation mystique** which is typical of pre-literate societies, where an individual takes on the identity of a creature or object.

So is astrology a recurrence in modern guise of a "primitive mentality" which has been overlaid by a rational approach?

TOTEMS

The Sun-signs in particular can be seen as a **totemic system**, rooted in a myth-making mentality. Totems are natural objects, commonly animals, taken as an **emblem** of a clan or an individual. The "spirit-animal" may be given at birth or discovered with the help of the medicine man.

Totemism is rooted in subjective perception which categorizes nature and experience. It is shaped by the culture. For the Pawnee Indians, the elm tree is black and north-east; the poplar is white and south-west.

The anthropologist Claude Lévi-Strauss (b1908) calls this process of using these affinities **bricolage**. It is an odd-job, Jack-of-all-Trades, handyman logic.

Bricolage

The "doctrine of correspondences" is a survival of the bricoleur imagination, and astrology itself is a remnant of totemism. In Greek, the word Zodiac means "circle of animals". Through astrology columns, the mass of people identify with a totem. You are a Leo, your totem is the Lion.

Modern rationalism does not apply to the Totem. The designation of the same Sun-sign to a twelfth of the population, or the possibility of Sun-sign readings being true one day and not the next, is not a problem for the bricoleur. If the cap fits, wear it.

If astrology involves subjective meaning, and if it connects with myth-making and the symbolic attitude, then we move from astrology as science to the polar extreme: **astrology as divination**.

Forms of divination such as Tarot cards and the Chinese Book of Changes depend on the manipulation of a system of symbols. So is astrology equivalent to these systems? If we think it is, then the debate about astrology changes, and the science-astrology argument is shifted.

From a science perspective, this takes astrology out of physics and biology, and into the realm of parapsychology.

Astrology-as-divination is a **metaphoric mirror**. Horoscope factors are treated "as if" they are metaphors mirroring salient features of the subject of the horoscope.

This approach fits Jung's **synchronicity** and moves away from **causation** and stellar determinism. Other than light itself, there is no causal connection between a mirror and the things it shows. Furthermore, because it depends on symbolic associations, the metaphoric mirror of the world exists not literally but psychically, in the imaginal realm. There has to be someone who "sees" in this realm of images and looks into the mirror – the astrologer.

So can astrologers decide whether their practice is **divination** or some type of **science**? Is it **subjective** or is it **objective**? Is it poetry or physics? The either-or logic is a trap. There is enough evidence to locate features of astrology in **both** categories. If we get rigid in our definitions, they break down.

A pragmatic approach is to allow a double conception of astrological significance. **Natural astrology** covers objective phenomena such as electro-magnetic fields in the solar system, the Moon and organic rhythms, the ancient metal-planet affinities, and the statistical demonstrations of the Gauquelins. This level is amenable to scientific testing, but has little to say about any particular individual.

On the other hand, **Divinatory astrology** refers to our experience of symbolism. It covers the traditional category of "judicial astrology" – judgments from horoscopes – but describes the range of symbolic expression, from the Star of Bethlehem to the junkiest pop astrology. Like consciousness, life and love, this level of meaning eludes science.

Because it overflows all definitions, astrology is a difficult target for genuine critics, but equally it is frustrating to present logically for its proponents. When different astrologers theorize about their subject, it's like various explorers describing bits of an elephant they can feel in the dark. Astrology seems to belong to some other order of knowing things, barely conceivable in the modern world.

So where is astrology going at the turn of a new millennium?

It looks stronger than at any time in the last three centuries. The huge media-led growth in pop astrology feeds into a New Age mind-body-spirit movement which guarantees astrology a star role. There is also a spirit of cooperation in astrology's community, plus a recovery by astrologers of sources of their tradition, especially through the US-led "Project Hindsight" programme of translations.

as above, so below . . .

We return to the final mystery which inspires the practice of Astrology. However dimly glimpsed, this speaks of a profound reciprocal relation between humanity, time and an intelligent Cosmos. In the words of Marsilio Ficino:

SUPPLEMENT

Star Wars: Is there a 13th sign?

Most astrologers believe that the entries of Pluto into Sagittarius and Uranus into Aquarius in 1995-6 heralded a new millennium changeover – or meltdown – in religion and belief-systems. Because of its association with Uranus, the sky god, astrology has to be involved. Pluto made its first entry into the sign of Sagittarius on 17 January 1995. Three days later, astrologers got advance notice of a typhoon to come, with a co-ordinated media hype reporting the "discovery" of the 13th sign of the Zodiac, *Ophiuchus*. The press, TV and radio in a number of countries simultaneously took the bait.

So what are the facts? Modern astronomy recognizes eighty-eight **constellations** of background stars. The twelve constellations from which our zodiac **signs** take their names lie along the ecliptic, the Sun's path through the year. However, the zodiac signs are pegged to the Spring Equinox point, and by the phenomenon of *precession of the Equinoxes* they have slowly slipped back against the corresponding constellations (see p29-32, also p114-5).

The constellation Ophiuchus is associated with the Greek mythological healer Aesclepius. His feet poke down onto the ecliptic between the constellations of Scorpio and Sagittarius, with a span of 18½ degrees. The Sun passes through the constellation of Ophiuchus between November 30th and December 18th each year.

Because Ophiuchus constitutes a 13th **constellation** on the ecliptic, by analogy it is suggested that we ought also to have a 13th **sign**. But this is disingenuous because – as astronomers obviously know – the Zodiac Signs are by definition twelve 30 degree sectors of the ecliptic measured from the Spring Equinox point.

The merit of Ophiuchus for the anti-astrologer is that:

a) popular confusion is introduced by giving everyone new dates of their "sign", as if these should be based on the Sun's movement through the constellations rather than through the 30 degree signs;

b) the well-rooted zodiac of twelve signs is broken up by a thirteenth, thus throwing the whole symbolism into doubt.

Ophiuchus is a neat package of (dis)information which is "rediscovered" every few years. This is only one of various instances where astrology's opponents prefer propaganda to intelligent inquiry.

Where to go next

For a wealth of world-wide information on astrological societies, schools, publications, chart services and software there is an invaluable free Annual Guide published by the **Urania Trust, 396 Caledonian Road, London N1 1DN, England**.

Geoffrey Cornelius and Maggie Hyde are both members of the **Company of Astrologers**, a non-profit body founded in London in 1983. The COA offers courses from beginner to advanced level, and runs correspondence courses, an annual residential weekend and a summer school. It also has a list of consultants and a chart calculation service. For further details send s.a.e. (or postal coupon if outside UK or Eire) to **Company of Astrologers, 6 Queen Square, London WC1N 3AR.**

Learning astrology

In this book, we haven't shown you how to set up the birthchart yourself because chart calculation services are widely available and cheap. However, if you want to learn astrology there may be classes in your area – check the Urania Trust guide and inquire at your Library. Correspondence courses and summer schools are also offered by various astrological schools.

Finding an astrologer

If you want an astrological consultation, recommendation by a friend is often best. Check out with the astrologer what he or she offers – most are happy to refer you to a colleague if they do not provide the exact service you want. Several schools have lists of astrologers who hold their qualification and subscribe to their code of practice.

Regulation of Astrology

Astrology usually operates outside state regulation, so anybody can set themselves up as a teacher or a consultant. In practice most countries have one or two major bodies or schools that are widely recognized. In the UK, leading organizations and reputable schools are represented on the **Advisory Panel on Astrological Education (APAE).**

Little Dictionary

Angle: the Angles of the Midheaven (MC) and Lower Heaven (IC, Imum Coeli), are the meeting point of the Ecliptic and the local Meridian. The Angles of the Ascendant and Descendant are the meeting point of Ecliptic and local Horizon (p84-85). They are the cusps of the Angular Houses 1, 4, 7, 10. Planets placed on or within a few degrees of these points are especially prominent in the horoscope.

Ascendant: the degree of the Zodiac which appears on the eastern horizon in the horoscope (p84-5).

Aspects: the arc or distance in degrees between any two planets or points in the Zodiac. The **orb** is the number of degrees allowed on either side of an exact aspect for the aspect still to be operative. An aspect is **applying** - still to be made - if it reaches exactitude in the hours or days after the time of the horoscope. It is **separating** if it was exact earlier. In horary, applying aspects show future events, separating aspects show the past. For aspects and aspect patterns, see p75-79.

Asteroids: a belt of vast numbers of fragments, believed to be a disintegrated planet, between the orbits of Mars and Jupiter. Ephemerides of some of the well-known asteroids have been published, especially for Ceres, Pallas, Juno and Vesta. Critics suggest that the use of asteroids symbolises a disintegration of astrological interpretation.

Chaldean Order: as viewed geocentrically (from the earth), the order of the planets in their apparent distances, and their consequent speeds of motion. The Chaldean Order refers only to the traditional planets, Saturn to Moon (p14).

Chiron: ⚷ a planetoid, possibly a trapped comet, between the orbits of Saturn and Uranus. Ephemerides of Chiron have been published and it has been taken up with enthusiasm by some astrologers, who suggest that it symbolises the wounded healer. Chiron is resisted by many traditionalists. As with the **asteroids** the argument is not fundamentally about whether Chiron 'works', since every factor conceivable by an astrologer is capable of generating valid symbolism.

Chronocrators: the "Markers of Time" in traditional astrology, Jupiter and Saturn. The 20-year Jupiter-Saturn conjunctions stay for around 200 years in the same element, forming an 800-year zodiac cycle. These cycles mark the spirit of the age (p136).

Correspondences: the ancient **theory of correspondences** follows the maxim, "As Above, So Below". All earthly matters below (the microcosm) correspond in their essential natures with a key principle or idea of the heavens above (the macrocosm). The human being is a complete microcosm.

Cusps: the point in the Zodiac which separates one house of the horoscope from another. There are therefore twelve cusps, one per house, but four of them form the **Angles** of the horoscope. The remaining eight are cusps of intermediate houses, between the angles (2,3,5,6,8,9,11 & 12).

Dignity: planets placed in signs they **rule**, or in which they are **exalted**, are in dignity and their influence is strengthened. They are in debility and weakened in signs opposite to their rulership (**detriment**) or opposite their exaltation (**fall**) (p 72-73). **Accidental Dignities and Debilities** refer to additional significant placings eg in the fortunate 10th house, conjunct the Part of Fortune etc. Traditional astrology employs a range of lesser dignities. These include triplicities (planets associated with elements), terms (minor subdivisions of each sign), and faces (ten degree divisions of signs, similar to decanates).

Directions: methods for timing events by moving ("directing") planets and other factors into new positions and aspects in the horoscope. This movement may be derived from the diurnal rotation of the earth/sky in the hours after birth (Primary Directions), or from planetary motions along the ecliptic in the days after birth (Secondary Directions or Progressions). As a modern development of the technique, the MC is progressed by the 'solar arc' (see below). Secondaries are simple to use but potent, and have become the leading method in modern practice. They are used in this book, see p109-11. There are various subsidiary techniques:

- **Solar Arc Directions** add the arc of the Sun's secondary progression for a given date to all other horoscope factors. This method is common in U.S. astrology.
- **Tertiary Directions** count lunar months after birth as equating to years of life.
- **Symbolic Directions** add fixed increments to horoscope factors for each year. They are called "symbolic" because the increment is not directly derived from astronomical movements. The most common usage applies one degree for each year. Traditional horary employs a type of symbolic direction so that one degree equates with a year, month or day, depending on context.

Elements: fire, earth, air and water are the four fundamental natures into which the twelve zodiac signs are divided (p53). A count of the distribution of the seven traditional planets amongst the elements indicates the horoscope's element balance, or a dominant or missing element. The element of the Ascendant also adds to the picture. A completely missing element is often compensated for through friends and the marriage partner, eg. no earth, friends or partners may have a prominence of earth.

Ephemeris: (plural ephemerides). A publication listing planetary positions and other information such as latitude, declination and sidereal time (star time), on a daily basis, usually for 0h or 12h at Greenwich. This information is essential in order to cast the horoscope.

Glastonbury Zodiac: discovered by Katharine Maltwood in 1925, is believed by its proponents to be the Round Table of King Arthur. It consists of zodiacal figures reflected in geographic features, place names and local lore in a 10-mile circle around Glastonbury in England. Other similar land formations have been proposed, notably that around Kingston-upon-Thames.

Harmonics: a mathematically based theory of astrology developed in the twentieth century in the UK by John Addey. The principle factors underlying the horoscope - signs, houses and aspects - are seen as measures of wave-forms in celestial circles, such as the ecliptic (signs), the diurnal cycle of the earth's rotation (houses) and planetary cycles (aspects). The wave forms express numbers. For example, the trine aspect is the division of the circle by 3, the four angles express the number 4. The method is then extended in horoscope analysis to harmonics not employed in conventional astrology (eg 5th, 7th, 9th, 25th harmonics). John Addey had some success in using the theory to reinterpret the Gauquelin findings, which display obvious wave forms.

Horary: a horoscope for the time and place that an astrologer is asked a specific question (p120-125).

Horoscope: a diagram of the heavens cast for a particular time and place, showing the Zodiac, planets, the rising and culminating signs and the twelve houses. It is variously referred to as a chart, map or figure. See Primer p81-5.

Houses: seen from any position on the earth the heavens divide naturally into four **quadrants** (eastern horizon to upper meridian, upper meridian to western horizon, and two comparable quadrants beneath the horizon). Each quadrant is trisected producing a total of twelve Houses of the horoscope (p82-5; meanings of houses p86). The **Table of Houses** lists the degrees rising on the Ascendant and culminating on the Midheaven, along with intermediate house cups, at four minute intervals over the 24-hour diurnal cycle. It is published for various geographical latitudes.

Katarche: the astrology of initiatives, including horary, decumbiture, elections and inceptions. These charts are all cast for a moment other than the birth moment with a view to considering what initiative in the situation can best be taken.

Mid-Points: a technique developed originally in modern German astrology. The middle point in the zodiac between any two planets or horoscope factors expresses the energies of those factors. The method usually dispenses with zodiac signs and intermediate houses. A common synastry method based on this approach is the **composite chart** where the midpoint is found for each planet and cusp between two horoscopes (eg each person's Sun is midpointed, then their Moons etc). The composite symbolises the relationship.

Mundane Astrology: the study of world events using planetary cycles and horoscopes for nations, events and political leaders (p134-7).

Mutual Reception: two planets, each placed in each other's sign of rulership, eg Jupiter in Cancer, the Moon in Sagittarius (p80).

Nodes: the intersection of a planet's orbit through the Earth-Sun orbital plane of the ecliptic. Only the **Moon's Nodes** are used in ordinary astrology (p80). Solar and lunar eclipses occur due to an earth-sun-moon-node alignment on the plane of the ecliptic.

Part of Fortune: parts or lots are theoretical positions in the zodiac, produced by an equation involving three symbolically appropriate factors, at least one of which is usually a cusp. The Arabs developed many Parts such as the Part of Marriage and the Part of Death. The Part of Fortune, or Fortuna, goes back to early astrology and has remained in regular use. It is calculated by the Ascendant, plus Moon, minus Sun. This places the part of Fortune as many degrees on in the Zodiac from the Ascendant, as the Moon is from the Sun. It is fortunate because it combines the powers of the Sun and Moon and brings them down to the earth through the horizon (Ascendant). The glyph for the Part of Fortune is also used in astronomy to show the Earth ⊕.

Progressions: one of the most important of the timing measures or **directions**, in which planets' positions each day after birth symbolise conditions in each year of life. Used both to confirm the astrologer's understanding of the symbolism in past events and to predict future developments (p109-111).

Rectification: adjusting the stated birth time to arrive at a time of birth which works as well as possible. This process is particularly necessary when the time of birth is not known within half an hour, or is not known at all. The horoscope is tested with appropriate timing measures to reveal major past events in life. An ancient technique which is still used is the **Pre-Natal Epoch** (or Trutine of Hermes). This involves finding a moment as the birth time which interchanges the degree of the Ascendant or Descendant at birth with the position of the Moon ten lunar months before birth, as well as interchanging the Asc. or Desc. ten lunar months earlier with the Moon of birth. This was originally believed to coincide with conception.

Relocation: the birthchart is re-cast for any place of importance to the individual in order to show his or her potential in that place (p128).

Retrograde: the apparent backwards motion of planets through the zodiac (p51 & p80).

Returns: the return of any planet to the position in the zodiac which it occupied at birth (p102).

Synastry: comparison of two or more charts with a view to their compatibility (p132). A symbolic **composite chart** of a relationship can also be derived from the midpoints of common factors between two horoscopes.

Transits: an aspect by a planet currently in the sky with a planet or other factor in a horoscope (p107-8). Transits often trigger into operation underlying timing factors such as progressions.